Anonymous

Acts and Statutes

Made in Parliament begun at Dublin, the twenty-second Day of October, Anno. etc.

Anonymous

Acts and Statutes
Made in Parliament begun at Dublin, the twenty-second Day of October, Anno. etc.

ISBN/EAN: 9783337067458

Printed in Europe, USA, Canada, Australia, Japan

Cover: Foto ©ninafisch / pixelio.de

More available books at **www.hansebooks.com**

ACTS
AND
STATUTES,

MADE

In a PARLIAMENT begun at *Dublin*, the Twenty-second Day, of *October*, *Anno Dom.* 1761, in the First Year of the Reign of our Most Gracious Sovereign Lord King *GEORGE* the Third.

BEFORE

His Excellency *Dunk*, Earl of *Halifax*, Lord Lieutenant General, and General Governor of *Ireland*.

DUBLIN:

Printed by BOULTER GRIERSON, Printer to the King's Most Excellent Majesty. MDCCLXII.

THE

CONTENTS

OF THE

FIRST SESSION

OF

King GEORGE III.

CHAP. I.

AN Act for granting and continuing to His Majesty, an additional Duty on Beer, Ale, Strong Waters, Wine, Tobacco, Hides, and other Goods and Merchandizes therein mentioned; and for prohibiting the Importation of Gold and Silver Lace, except of the Manufacture of *Great Britain*.

Page 3

The CONTENTS.

CHAP. II.

An Act for granting to His Majesty a further additional Duty on Wine, Silk, Hops, China, Earthen, Japanned, Lacquered Ware, and Vinegar, and for better securing the Repayment of One Hundred and Fifty Thousand Pounds, paid into the Treasury for the Support of His Majesty's Government, pursuant to an Act of the last Session, together with the Interest thereof; and for securing the Repayment of such Sums of Money, not exceeding in the Whole the Sum of Three Hundred Thousand Pounds, as have been, or shall be paid into the Treasury, or shall be advanced to His present Majesty, pursuant to the Resolutions of the House of Commons, the last Session of Parliament, together with the Interest thereof.
Page 29

CHAP. III.

An Act to perpetuate, with Amendments, a Clause in an Act passed in the Ninth Year of His late Majesty King *George* the Second, Intituled, *An Act for the more effectual assigning of Judgments, and for the more speedy Recovery of Rents by Distress.* Page 47

CHAP.

The CONTENTS.

CHAP. IV.

An Act for allowing further Time to Persons in Offices or Employments, to qualify themselves, pursuant to an Act, Intituled, *An Act to prevent the further Growth of Popery.*
Page 53

CHAP. V.

An Act for granting to His Majesty, the several Duties, Rates, and Impositions, therein expressed, to be applied to pay an Interest, at the Rate of Five Pounds *per Centum per Annum*, for the several Sums therein provided for, and towards the Discharge of the said Principal Sums. 59

CHAP. VI.

An Act for Licensing Hawkers and Pedlars, and for Encouragement of *English* Protestant Schools. 87

CHAP. VII.

An Act for continuing and amending an Act, Intituled, *An Act for better regulating the Collection of His Majesty's Revenue, and for preventing Frauds therein*; and for repealing an Act

The CONTENTS.

Act made the laſt Seſſion of Parliament, Intituled, *An Act for continuing and amending ſeveral Laws heretofore made, relating to His Majeſty's Revenue, and for the more effectual preventing of Frauds in His Majeſty's Cuſtoms and Excife, and the ſeveral Acts and Statutes which are mentioned in the ſaid Act, and continued thereby.* 103

CHAP. VIII.

An Act to enable Tenants for Life to make perpetual Leaſes of Grounds whereon to erect publick Hoſpitals. 127

CHAP. IX.

An Act to prevent the counterfeiting Gold and Silver Lace, and for ſettling and adjuſting the Proportions of fine Gold, Silver, and Silk, and for the better making of Gold and Silver Thread. 131

CHAP. X.

An Act to prevent the exceſſive Price of Coals in the City of *Dublin*. 141

CHAP.

The CONTENTS.

CHAP. XI.

An Act to prevent Abuses committed by Justices of Peace, acting under the Charters of Cities and Towns Corporate.   157

CHAP. XII.

An Act for the Security of Protestant Purchasers.   163

CHAP. XIII.

An Act for quieting the Possessions of Protestants, deriving under Converts from the Popish Religion.   169

CHAP. XIV.

An Act for preventing Frauds and Abuses in the vending, preparing, and administring Drugs and Medicines.   175

CHAP. XV.

An Act for altering and amending an Act of Parliament passed in the Seventh Year of

The CONTENTS.

the Reign of His late Majesty King *George* the Second, Intituled, *An Act for repairing the Road leading from the Bridge over the* Bann-Water, *commonly called the* Bann-Bridge, *in the County of* Down, *to the Town of* Belfast, *in the County of* Antrim.   Page 201

CHAP. XVI.

An Act for the Relief of Insolvent Debtors.
229

CHAP. XVII.

An Act for reviving, continuing, and amending several temporary Statutes, and for other Purposes therein mentioned.   277

CHAP. XVIII.

An Act for the more easy and equal assessing and applotting all Money presented by the Grand Jury of each Assizes to be held for the City, and County of the City of *Cork,* and for putting the Coaches, Chaises, Chairs, and Sedans, that ply for Hire in the said City, under the like Regulations, for the Benefit of the Workhouse of *Cork,* as they are in *Dublin,* and also for the better regulating the Harbour of *Cork.*
307

CHAP.

CHAP. XIX.

An Act for building a Stone Bridge from the Quay opposite *Prince's-Street*, in the City of *Cork*, to *Lavit's-Island*, and a Stone Bridge from thence to the *Red Abbey Marsh*, with a Draw Bridge or Lifting Bridge of Wood in the Center of the latter, sufficient to let Vessels pass and repass, and also for supplying the said City with Water. Page 337

Private Bills.

An Act for rectifying a Mistake in the Marriage Settlement of *Francis Pierpoint Burton*, Esquire, with *Elizabeth*, his present Wife, and for vesting the said *Francis Pierpoint Burton*'s Estate in the County of *Limerick*, in him the said *Francis Pierpoint Burton*, his Heirs and Assigns, for ever.

An Act for incorporating the Trustees of *Wilson*'s Hospital, in the County of *Westmeath*, and for other Purposes mentioned therein.

The CONTENTS.

An Act to enable *Henry Croker*, Esquire, to make Leases of his Estate for three Lives, or thirty-one Years, at a full improved Rent, and to charge his Estate with a Jointure for any Wife he shall marry, not exceeding Two Hundred Pounds by the Year.

An Act for confirming and establishing an Agreement made between Sir *Edward King*, Baronet, and *Henry King*, Esquire, concerning the real and personal Estates, whereof *Robert*, late Lord *Kingsborough*, died seized or possessed, and for making the said Agreement effectual, and for raising a sufficient Sum of Money for discharging the Debts and Incumbrances affecting the same, and other Purposes.

An Act for vesting certain Lands, Tenements, and Hereditaments, situate in the County of *Tipperary*, in the Kingdom of *Ireland*, the Estate of *Philip Percival*, Esquire, in Trustees, in order that the same may be sold for the Payment of Debts, and other Incumbrances affecting the same; and also the Estate of the said *Philip Percival*, situate in the County of *Sligo*, in the Kingdom of *Ireland*, and for the purchasing of other Lands more contiguous to the Estate of the said *Philip Percival*, situate in the County of *Sligo*,

to

The CONTENTS.

to be settled to the same Uses as the said *Sligo* Estate now stands limited.

An Act for explaining, amending, and carrying more effectually into Execution an Act, Intituled, *An Act for the Relief of the Creditors of* of Daniel Reddy, *Esquire, and* Dudley Reddy, *his Brother, deceased, by Sale of their Real and Personal Estates, for Payment of their Debts.*

An Act for vesting several Lands, Tenements, and Hereditaments in the Counties of *Galway* and *Mayo*, late the Estate of *Robert Blake* of *Ardfry*, Esquire, deceased, and of *Richard Blake* his Son, deceased, in Trustees, for Sale of a competent Part thereof, for Payment of Debts and Incumbrances affecting the same, and for settling the Residue thereof, to and for the several Uses, Intents, and Purposes therein mentioned.

An Act for vesting the Estate of *Robert Hickman*, late of *Barntick* in the County of *Clare*, Esquire, deceased, in Trustees, to be sold for Payment of the Debts and Incumbrances affecting the same, and for applying the surplus Purchase-Money, or such Part of the said Estate as shall remain unsold, according to the Intention of the said *Robert Hickman*'s Will.

The CONTENTS.

An Act to enables *Charles Mofs*, during his Minority, and in cafe of his Death without Iffue, to enable *Jane Mofs*, during her Minority, by and with the Confent of their Guardians, to make Leafes for Lives or Years of certain Plots or Pieces of Ground in the County of *Dublin*, and County of the City of *Dublin*, and that fuch Leafes, being made without Fine, and at the beft and higheft Rent, may be good againft all Perfons.

AN ACT

FOR

Granting and Continuing to His Majesty, an additional Duty on Beer, Ale, Strong Waters, Wine, Tobacco, Hides, and other Goods and Merchandizes therein mentioned; and for prohibiting the Importation of all Gold and Silver Lace, except of the Manufacture of *Great Britain*.

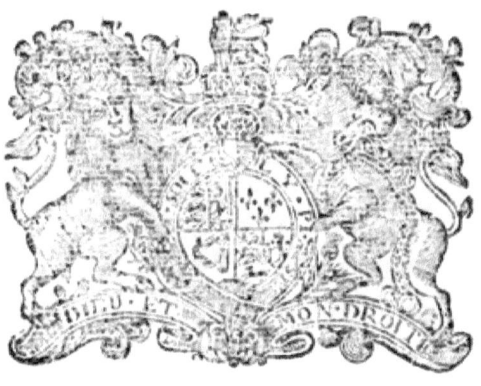

DUBLIN:

Printed by BOULTER GRIERSON, Printer to the King's Most Excellent Majesty. MDCCLXII.

AN ACT

FOR

Granting and Continuing to His Majesty, an Additional Duty on Beer, Ale, Strong Waters, Wine, Tobacco, Hides, and other Goods and Merchandizes therein mentioned; and for prohibiting the Importation of all Gold and Silver Lace, except of the Manufacture of *Great Britain*.

CHAP. I.

WE your Majesty's most Dutiful and Loyal Subjects, the Commons of Ireland, in Parliament Assembled, having a just Sense of your Royal Care for the Prosperity of all your Subjects, and well knowing that the Security of this your Realm, and the Continuance of the many Blessings we enjoy under

Chap. I. under Your mild and auspitious Reign, depend on the Support of Your Majesty's Government, do most humbly beseech Your Majesty, that it may be Enacted;

And be it Enacted by the King's Most Excellent Majesty, by and with the Advice and Consent of the Lords Spiritual and Temporal, and Commons in this present Parliament assembled, and by the Authority of the same, that the several and respective Duties and Impositions on Beer, Ale, Strong Waters, Wine, Tobacco, and other Goods and Merchandizes, which in and by an Act of Parliament made and passed in the first Year of the Reign of His late Majesty King George the Second, Intitled, An Act for Granting to His Majesty an Additional Duty on Beer, Ale, Strong Waters, Wine, Tobacco, and other Goods and Merchandizes therein mentioned; and also a Tax on Salaries, Profits of Employments, Fees, and Pensions, and for securing the Repayment of Fifty Thousand Pounds Sterling, formerly advanced to His late Majesty for the Use of the Publick, together with the Interest thereof, were Granted and Continued unto His said late Majesty King George the Second, or chargeable in Manner therein mentioned, from the Twenty Fifth Day of March, One thousand seven hundred and twenty

twenty eight, to the Twenty Fifth Day of December, One thousand seven hundred and twenty nine inclusive, and which by one other Act made and passed in the Third Year of His said late Majesty's Reign, Intitled, An Act for Granting and Continuing to His Majesty an additional Duty on Beer, Ale, Strong Waters, Wine, Tobacco, and other Goods and Merchandizes therein mentioned; were Continued until the Twenty Fifth Day of December, in the Year of Our Lord, One thousand seven hundred and thirty one inclusive, and which were further Granted and Continued from Time to Time by subsequent Acts of Parliament made in this Kingdom, until the Twenty Fifth Day of December, in the Year of Our Lord One thousand seven hundred and sixty one inclusive, except the Duty of Five Shillings thereby Imposed upon every Gallon of Brandy or Spirits above Proof, be further Granted, Continued, Raised, Collected, Levied, and Paid unto Your Majesty, Your Heirs, and Successors, from the Twenty Fifth Day of December, One thousand seven hundred and sixty one, until the Twenty Fifth Day of December, One thousand seven hundred and sixty three inclusive.

And be it further Enacted by the Authority aforesaid, That in Lieu of the said excepted

Chap. I. cepted Duty of five Shillings a Gallon upon all Brandy and Spirits above Proof, an additional Duty be laid on all Foreign Spirits (above the Quality of single Spirits) which shall be Imported into this Kingdom, from the Twenty fifth Day of December, One thousand seven hundred and sixty one, to the Twenty fifth Day of December, One thousand seven hundred and sixty three inclusive; which said additional Duty shall be payable for such Spirits and shall be charged thereon in Proportion to the Duties payable for single Spirits of the same Denomination, according to the Comparative Degree of Strength which such Spirits, so to be imported, shall bear to single Spirits of the same Denomination.

And be it further Enacted by the Authority aforesaid, That all and Singular the said Duties hereby Granted and Continued, shall be Raised, Levied, Collected, and paid unto Your Majesty, Your Heirs, and Successors during the Term aforesaid, over and above all other Duties payable for the same, by Virtue of an Act made in this Kingdom, in the Fourteenth and Fifteenth Years of the Reign of King Charles the Second, Intitled, An Act for the settling the Excise or New Impost upon His Majesty, His Heirs and Successors, according to the Book of Rates therein

Georgii Tertii Regis. 7

therein inserted; or by Virtue of one other
Act, made in the Fourteenth and Fifteenth
Years of the Reign of the said King Charles
the Second, Intituled, An Act for Settling the
Subsidy of Poundage, and Granting a Subsidy of
Tunnage, and other Sums of Money, unto His
Royal Majesty, His Heirs and Successors, the same
to be paid upon Merchandizes imported and exported into or out of the Kingdom of *Ireland*, according to the Book of Rates hereunto annexed.

CHAP.
I.

Provided always, and be it further Enacted by the Authority aforesaid, That if the said Wines, Strong Waters, Spirits perfectly made, and Spirits made and distilled of Wine and Brandy, or Spirits above the Quality of Single Spirits, upon which the said additional Duties are Charged, shall, after Payment thereof, or Security given for the same, be again Exported by any Merchant or Merchants, that is or are a Subject or Subjects of this Realm, or any other of Your Majesty's Dominions, within Twenty Four Kalendar Months, or by Merchant Strangers, within Twelve Kalendar Months after the Importation thereof, and due Proof first made, by Certificate from the Proper Officer, of the due Entry of such Wines, Strong Waters, Spirits perfectly made, and Spirits made and Distilled of Wine, Brandy, or Spirits

B 2 above

CHAP. I. above the Quality of Single Spirits, and of the Payment of the said additional Duties hereby Granted and Charged thereon, or Security being given for the same, and that all other Requisites have been performed, which are by Law required to be performed in Cases where the Duties of Excise are to be repaid by Virtue of the before mentioned Act, Intitled, An Act for the Settling of the Excise or New Impost upon His Majesty, His Heirs, and Successors, according to the Book of Rates therein inserted; that then the said additional Duties shall, without any Delay or Reward, be paid, or allowed unto such Merchant or Merchants so Exporting the same, within one Month after Demand thereof, or the Security for the said additional Duties by this Act charged, shall be vacated or discharged, as to so much thereof as shall be so Exported; any thing herein contained to the contrary notwithstanding.

And be it further Enacted by the Authority aforesaid, That for a further Supply to Your Majesty, the further Additional Duty of Twenty Shillings, Sterling, on every Hundred Weight of Molasses, and the further Additional Duty of Twenty Shillings Sterling, on every Hundred Weight of Treacle, which in and by the said Act of Parliament, made in the First Year of the

the Reign of his said late Majesty King George the Second, were Granted unto his said late Majesty, from the Twenty fifth Day of March, Which was in the Year of Our Lord, One thousand seven hundred and twenty eight, until the Twenty fifth Day of December, One thousand seven hundred and twenty nine, inclusive; and Which were further Granted and Continued unto His said late Majesty, from Time to Time, by other Acts of Parliament, made in this Kingdom, from the said Twenty fifth Day of December, One thousand seven hundred and twenty nine, until the twenty fifth Day of December, One thousand seven hundred and sixty one inclusive, be further Granted, Continued, Collected, Raised, Levied, and Paid unto Your Majesty, Your Heirs and Successors, from the said twenty fifth Day of December, One thousand seven hundred and sixty one, until the twenty fifth Day of December, One thousand seven hundred and sixty three, inclusive.

And be it further Enacted by the Authority aforesaid, That for and towards a further Supply to Your Majesty, an Additional Duty of Six Pence per Yard, for and upon all Foreign Stuffs called Romalls, and all Manufactures made of Cotton, or of Cotton and Linen mixed,

whether

Whether plain, painted, or stained, which shall be Imported into this Kingdom from any Parts beyond the Seas (except the Manufacture of Great Britain) and also an Additional Duty of Six Pence per Yard, over and above the present Duties, for all Cambricks, not of the Manufacture of Great Britain, which shall be Imported into this Kingdom, exceeding a Yard Wide, shall be Raised, Levied, Collected, and paid unto Your Majesty, Your Heirs and Successors, from the Twenty fifth Day of December, One thousand seven hundred and sixty one, to the Twenty fifth Day of December, One thousand seven hundred and sixty three, inclusive.

And be it further Enacted by the Authority aforesaid, That a further Additional Duty of Three Pence per Yard upon all Cambricks and Lawns, not of the Manufacture of Great Britain, which shall be Imported into this Kingdom, from and after the Twenty fifth Day of December, One thousand seven hundred and sixty one, shall be Raised, Levied, Collected, and paid to Your Majesty, Your Heirs and Successors, from the said Twenty fifth Day of December, One thousand seven hundred and sixty one, to the Twenty fifth Day of December, One thousand seven hundred and

and sixty three, inclusive, over and above all other Duties payable for the same.

And be it further Enacted by the Authority aforesaid, That a further Additional Duty of Three Pence per Yard, upon all Cambricks and Lawns, other than such as are of the Manufacture of Great Britain, which shall be Imported into this Kingdom, from and after the Twenty fifth Day of December, One thousand seven hundred and sixty one, shall be Raised, Levied, Collected, and Paid to Your Majesty, Your Heirs and Successors, from the said Twenty fifth Day of December, One thousand seven hundred and sixty one, to the Twenty fifth Day of December, One thousand seven hundred and sixty three, inclusive, over and above all other Duties payable for the same.

And be it further Enacted by the Authority aforesaid, That for a further Supply to Your Majesty, an additional Duty of Six Pence per Hide, for and upon every raw and untanned Hide, which shall be Exported out of this Kingdom, to Parts beyond the Seas (Except Great Britain) shall be Raised, Levied, Collected, and paid unto Your Majesty, Your Heirs and Successors, from the Twenty fifth Day of December,

CHAP. I. One thousand seven hundred and sixty one, to the Twenty Fifth Day of December, One thousand seven hundred and sixty three, inclusive.

And be it further Enacted by the Authority aforesaid, That for a further Supply to Your Majesty, an additional Duty of One Shilling per Rheam of Paper (over and above the Duties now payable thereon) shall be Levied, Raised, and Paid unto Your Majesty, Your Heirs, and Successors, upon all Paper imported into this Kingdom (Except of the Manufacture of Great Britain) provided such Paper exceeds Five Shillings in value per Rheam, from the Twenty Fifth Day of December, One thousand seven hundred and sixty one, to the Twenty Fifth Day of December, One thousand seven hundred and sixty three, inclusive.

And be it further Enacted by the Authority aforesaid, That the additional Rates and Duties on Coffee, Tea, Chocolate, and Cocoa Nuts, Granted and Continued by the said Act, in the first Year of the Reign of His said late Majesty King George the Second, and which were from Time to Time, afterwards further Continued by several subsequent Acts of Parliament, and

all

all Money arising thereby, shall be paid to the Trustees appointed for the Management of the Hempen and Flaxen Manufactures of this Kingdom, to be by them applied to encourage and support the said Manufactures, and the Trade thereof in this Kingdom; and that the said additional Duties on raw and untanned Hides, and all Money arising thereby, shall be paid to the said Trustees, to be by them applied toward encouraging the raising of Flax-Seed in this Kingdom; and that the said last mentioned further additional Duty of three Pence per Yard upon all Cambricks and Lawns, and all Money arising thereby, shall be paid and applied to the Use of the Governor and Company for carrying on the Cambrick Manufacture in Dundalk, or elsewhere in this Kingdom.

And be it further Enacted by the Authority aforesaid, That all and every the several and respective additional Duties hereby Granted or Continued, shall be Raised, Answered, Collected, and Paid unto Your Majesty, Your Heirs, and Successors, during the Term aforesaid, at the same Time, and in like Manner, and by such Ways, Means, and Methods, and by such Rules and Directions, and under such Penalties and Forfeitures, and with such Powers, as are
D   appointed,

CHAP. I. appointed, directed, and expressed, in and by the said Act, made in this Kingdom, in the Fourteenth and Fifteenth Years of the Reign of King Charles the Second, Intitled, An Act for the Settling of the Excise or New Impost upon His Majesty, His Heirs and Successors, according to the Book of Rates therein inserted; or by any other Law now in Force, relating to the Revenue of Excise in this Kingdom, as fully and effectually, to all Intents and Purposes, as if the same were particularly mentioned, expressed, and enacted again in the Body of this present Act; With like Remedy of Appeal, to and for the Party grieved, as in and by the said Act of Excise, or any other Law or Laws now in being, relating to the Duties of Excise is provided.

And be it further Enacted by the Authority aforesaid, That the Six Pence per Pound, and all other Fees, which shall or may be payable to the Vice-Treasurer, or Vice-Treasurers, Pay-Master, or Receiver-General, for, or on Account of, or out of the Aids hereby Granted unto Your Majesty, other than, and except such part thereof, as is herein after appointed to be paid to the Trustees of the Hempen and Flaxen Manufactures of this Kingdom, shall be received by the said Vice-Treasurer

or

or Vice-Treasurers, Receiver, or Paymaster General, for the Use of Your Majesty, Your Heirs and Successors, during the Term aforesaid, and shall be duly accounted for by him or them to Your Majesty, Your Heirs and Successors, as a further and additional Aid hereby given and granted.

And be it further Enacted by the Authority aforesaid, That the several Sums herein after mentioned, be paid out of the aforesaid Additional Duties and Aids Granted and Continued to Your Majesty by this present Act, to the Persons hereinafter mentioned, that is to say, The Sum of Two Thousand Pounds, per Annum, for two Years, from the Twenty fifth Day of December, One thousand seven hundred and sixty one, to the Twenty fifth Day of December, One thousand seven hundred and sixty three, inclusive, to the Trustees appointed for the Management of the Hempen and Flaxen Manufactures of this Kingdom, for Encouraging and Raising sufficient Quantities of Hemp and Flax in this Kingdom; and also the further Sum of Two Thousand Pounds, per Annum, for two Years, from the said Twenty fifth Day of December, One thousand seven hundred and sixty one, to the said Twenty fifth Day of December, One thousand seven hundred

CHAP. I. hundred and sixty three, inclusive, to the said Trustees, appointed for the Management of the Hempen and Flaxen Manufactures of this Kingdom, for the Encouragement of the said Hempen and Flaxen Manufactures in the Provinces of Leinster, Munster, and Connaught, freed and discharged from the Payment of Six Pence per Pound, and all other Fees which shall or may be payable to the Vice-Treasurer, Receiver, or Paymaster-General of this Kingdom, Clerk of the Pells, or any other Officer or Officers of this Kingdom; the Sum of Two Thousand Pounds to the Right Honourable the Speaker of the House of Commons, towards defraying his extraordinary Expences during this Session of Parliament; the Sum of Five Hundred Pounds to Agmondisham and George Vesey, Esquires, Accomptant-General, as a Reward for their Expence and Trouble in preparing and Stating the Publick Accounts of the Nation, laid before the House of Commons this Session of Parliament; the Sum of Five Hundred Pounds to Edward Sterling and Henry Alcock, Esquires, Clerks of the House of Commons, as a Reward for their Attendance and Service this Session of Parliament; the Sum of Two Hundred Pounds to Anthony Sterling, Clerk-Assistant, as a Reward for his Attendance and Service

vice this Session of Parliament; the Sum of Four Hundred and Twenty six Pounds, Thirteen Shillings and Four Pence, to James Baillie, Esquire, Serjeant at Arms, as a Reward for his Attendance and Service this Session of Parliament; the Sum of Three Hundred and Fifty Pounds to Benjamin Higgins and James Brown, the Clerks attending the Committee of Accounts, and the other Committees of the House of Commons, as a Reward for their Attendance and Service this Session of Parliament, to be equally divided between them; the Sum of One Hundred and Twelve Pounds to Abraham Bradley, for Printing the Publick Accounts laid before the House of Commons this Session of Parliament; the Sum of Fifty Pounds to Hulton Bradley, as a Reward for his Trouble and Attendance in delivering the Votes to the Members of the House of Commons this Session of Parliament; the Sum of Eighty Pounds to James Savage and Thomas Gilmore, Door-keepers to the House of Commons, as a Reward for their Attendance and Service this Session of Parliament, to be equally divided between them; the Sum of Four Thousand Pounds to the Corporation for Promoting and Carrying on an Inland Navigation in Ireland, towards making the River Nore navigable from the City of Kilkenny to Ennisteage,

CHAP. I. in the County of Kilkenny, to be by them accounted for to Parliament; the Sum of One Thousand Pounds to Sir Ralph Gore, Baronet, and Richard Dawson, Esquire, towards finishing the Church of Saint Thomas, in the Parish of Saint Thomas, in the City of Dublin, to be accounted for to Parliament; the Sum of Ten Thousand Pounds to the Corporation for Promoting and Carrying on an Inland Navigation in Ireland, to be by them Expended in carrying on the Grand Canal leading from Dublin to the Shannon, to be accounted for to Parliament; the Sum of Three Thousand Pounds to Thomas Eyre, Anthony Green, and George Martin, Esquires, for carrying on the Pier at Dunleary, to be accounted for to Parliament; the Sum of Twelve Thousand Pounds to the Incorporated Society for Promoting English Protestant Schools in Ireland; the Sum of One Thousand Pounds to the Vicar and Church-Wardens of the Parish of Saint Catharine, Dublin, to be applied by them towards Building the Church in said Parish, to be accounted for to Parliament; the Sum of Five Hundred Pounds to Thomas Barbon, Esquire, and the Reverend Doctor Edward Lyndon, to Compleat and Finish an Aqueduct from the River Finisk to the Town of Dungarvan, in the County of Waterford,

they

they giving sufficient Security for the due Execution of the Work, and to account for the said Sum to Parliament; the Sum of Two Thousand Pounds to the Most Honourable James, Marquis of Kildare, Charles, Earl of Drogheda, John, Earl of Wandesford, the Right Honourable Sir William Fownes, Baronet, the Right Honourable Benjamin Burton, Sir Richard Butler, Baronet, Thomas Butler, Maurice Keating, John Rochfort, Walter Weldon, James Agar the younger, John Gore, Beauchamp Bagenall, Robert Doyne, Ralph Gore, John Digby, Henry Bunbury, Elias Best, John Saintleger, William Stewart, George Hartpole, and William Browne, Esquires, or any Five of them, to be by them applied to remove the Obstructions in the Navigation of the River Barrow, from the Tide-Water at Saint Mullin's, to Monasterevan, to be accounted for to Parliament; the Sum of Two Thousand Pounds to the Corporation for Promoting and Carrying on an Inland Navigation in Ireland, to be by them applied towards Inclosing, Fixing, and Deepning the Channel of the River Boyne, from the Pile-Work, below the Bridge of Drogheda, to the Bar of said River, to be accounted for to Parliament; the Sum of One Thousand Five Hundred Pounds to Thomas Eyre and George Hamilton, Esquires, to be by them applied in Extending the Pier of Ballbriggan, in the Bay of Skerries, they giving Security for the due Execution of the Work, and to account for the said Sum to Parliament; the Sum of Four Thousand Pounds to Andrew Franklin, Esquire, Mayor, James Morrison and William Fitten, Esquires, Sheriffs of the City of Cork, and to Alderman Bradshaw, George and James Piercy, Hugh Lawton, Francis Carleton, James and Paul Benson, Thomas Strettle, and Christopher Carleton, all of the said City, Merchants, and to James Hartnet, Esquire, or any five of them, for Clearing and Improving the Channel of Cork Harbour, from the Custom-House Quay to a Place called Black Rock, to be accounted for to Parliament; the Sum of Four Thousand Five Hundred Pounds to the Commissioners appointed by Act of Parliament, for Widening and Repairing Baal's Bridge, in the City of Limerick, or to any five of them, for Continuing the New Quay Eastward, on the North Side of the River Shannon, to the Back River, and on the South Side, to the South Bank of the New Canal, and for Purchasing several Houses on the West Side of Baal's Bridge, and also two antient Mills, and for prostrating the Dams of the same, to be accounted for to Parliament; the Sum of Eight Thousand Pounds to the

Corporation

Corporation for Promoting and Carrying on an Inland Navigation in Ireland, to be by them applied towards making the River Shannon Navigable, from the City of Limerick to the Town of Killaloe, to be by them accounted for to Parliament; the Sum of One Thousand Eight Hundred and Fifty Pounds, Eight Shillings and Nine Pence, to the Corporation for Promoting and Carrying on an Inland Navigation in Ireland, to be by them applied to make and finish the Harbour of Wicklow, to be accounted for to Parliament; the Sum of Two Thousand Five Hundred Pounds to the Corporation for Promoting and Carrying on an Inland Navigation in Ireland, for making the River Black-water Navigable from Dromagh, in the County of Cork, to Cappoquin, in the County of Waterford, to be by them Accounted for to Parliament; the Sum of Five Thousand Pounds to the Lord Mayor, Sheriffs, Commons, and Citizens of the City of Dublin, towards Enabling them to continue the Ballast-Office Wall to the East End of the Piles, to be Accounted for to Parliament; the Sum of Four Thousand Two Hundred and Fifty Two Pounds to the Governors of the Work-House of the City of Dublin, towards Enabling them to discharge the Debt contracted by them on

CHAP. I.

Account

CHAP. I.

Account of the Foundling Children; the Sum of Three Thousand Pounds to the Governors and Guardians of the Hospital for the Relief of Poor Lying-in Women in Dublin, to enable them to discharge the Debts due on Account of the said Hospital, and to Finish and Furnish the same, to be accounted for to Parliament; the Sum of Four Thousand Pounds to the Corporation for Promoting and Carrying on an Inland Navigation in Ireland, to be by them applied towards making the River Lagan Navigable, and opening a Passage by Water from Loughneagh to the Town of Belfast, to be by them accounted for to Parliament; the Sum of Three Thousand Pounds to the Corporation for Promoting and Carrying on an Inland Navigation in Ireland, to be by them applied towards making a Navigable Canal from the Bason in Drumreagh, in the County of Tyrone, to Farlough-Lough in said County, to be accounted for to Parliament; the Sum of Two Thousand Five Hundred and Thirty Three Pounds, Sixteen Shillings and Eight Pence, to Edward Sterling, Esquire, the Cost due for Printing and Binding the Tenth and Eleventh Volumes of the Journals of the House of Commons, for the Use of the Members; the Sum of Three Hundred Pounds to Edward Sterling,

Sterling, Esquire, for his Care and Dispatch in preparing Copies of the said Two Volumes, and making Indexes to the same; the Sum of One Thousand Pounds to Jane Mosse, Widow of the late Doctor Bartholomew Mosse, for the Use of herself and her Children, in Consideration of the Merit of her late Husband, with regard to the Publick, by giving up his Time to the Care of the Hospital for the Relief of Poor Lying-in Women, and Superintending the Building to the Time of his Death, by which he hurt his Family in their Circumstances; the Sum of Five Hundred Pounds to George Semple, Engineer and Architect, for Building of Essex Bridge, in Consideration of his Merit in Executing the same with Extraordinary Care and Diligence, to the great Detriment of his Health, whereby he is rendered incapable to follow Business; the Sum of Two Thousand Pounds to Arthur Mervyn, Esquire, to Enable him to finish the Mill and Granaries by him begun at Naal, in the County of Meath, to be accounted for to Parliament; the Sum of One Hundred and Seventy Pounds to James Smythe, Esquire, and his Clerk, for Six Months Salary, for their Attendance and Trouble in paying the Premiums for the Inland Carriage of Corn to Dublin, from the first of November, One thousand seven hundred

CHAP. I.

hundred and fifty nine, to the first of May, One thousand seven hundred and sixty, the Sum of Seventy five Pounds to Mr. William Horton, for Examining the Premiums paid for Inland Carriage of Corn to Dublin, from the first of November, One thousand seven hundred and fifty nine, to the first of May, One thousand seven hundred and sixty; the Sum of One Thousand Pounds to William Colvill, Samuel Colvill, and Arthur Bryan, Merchants, to enable them to finish the Dry Dock at the West End of the North Wall, upon their giving Security to perform the said Work, and to account to Parliament; the Sum of two Thousand Pounds to the Dublin Society, for the Improvement of Husbandry, and other useful Arts, to enable them to continue their Premiums for the Reclaiming and Improving of Mountains and Boggy Lands, and in the Encouragement and Improvement of Agriculture and Manufactures, and also the Sum of Ten Thousand Pounds, to be by them distributed to such and so many of the several Persons who petitioned the House of Commons this Session of Parliament for Premiums or Rewards, and upon which Reports have been made, and in such Shares and Proportions, as the said Society shall think fit; all Which said

several

several Sums are to be paid by the Vice-Treasurers, or Receiver-General of this Kingdom, without any further or other Warrant to be sued for, had, or obtained in that behalf.

CHAP. I.

And be it further Enacted by the Authority aforesaid, That no Gold or Silver Lace whatsoever (except of the Manufacture of Great Britain) shall, from and after the Twenty fifth Day of December, One thousand seven hundred and sixty one, be Imported in any Ship or Vessel whatsoever, into this Kingdom, under the Penalty of the Forfeiture of all such Lace, and treble the Value thereof, and the Ship or Vessel in which the same shall be Imported, with all her Guns, Tackle, Furniture, Ammunition, and Apparel; One Moiety of which Forfeitures shall be and remain to Your Majesty, Your Heirs and Successors, and the other Moiety to him or them who shall Seize and Sue for the same, by Action, Bill, Plaint, or Information, in the Court of Exchequer, wherein no Wager of Law, Protection, Essoign, or other dilatory Plea, shall be allowed.

CHAP. II.

AN ACT

FOR

Granting to His Majesty a further Additional Duty on Wine, Silk, Hops, *China*, Earthen, Japanned, Lacquered Ware, and Vinegar, and for better securing the Repayment of One Hundred and Fifty Thousand Pounds, paid into the Treasury for the Support of His Majesty's Government, pursuant to an Act of the last Session, together with the Interest thereof; and for securing the Repayment of such Sums of Money, not exceeding in the Whole the Sum of Three Hundred Thousand Pounds, as have been, or shall be paid into the Treasury, or shall be advanced to His Present Majesty, pursuant to the Resolutions of the House of Commons, the last Session of Parliament, together with the Interest thereof.

DUBLIN:

Printed by BOULTER GRIERSON, Printer to the King's Most Excellent Majesty. MDCCLXII.

AN ACT
FOR

Granting to His Majesty a further Additional Duty on Wine, Silk, Hops, *China*, Earthen, Japanned, Lacquered Ware, and Vinegar, and for better securing the Repayment of One Hundred and Fifty Thousand Pounds, paid into the Treasury for the Support of His Majesty's Government, pursuant to an Act of the last Session, together with the Interest thereof; and for securing the Repayment of such Sums of Money, not exceeding in the Whole the Sum of Three Hundred Thousand Pounds, as have been, or shall be paid into the Treasury, or shall be advanced to His present Majesty, pursuant to the Resolutions of the House of Commons the last Session of Parliament, together with the Interest thereof.

CHAP. II.

WHEREAS by an Act passed in the last Session of Parliament, Intituled, An Act for Granting to His Majesty a further Additional Duty on Wine, Silk,

CHAP. II.

Silk, Hops, *China*, Earthen, Japanned, and Lacquered Ware, and Vinegar, to be applied to pay an Interest of Four Pounds *per Centum, per Annum*, for such Sums of Money, not exceeding in the Whole, the Sum of One Hundred and Fifty Thousand Pounds, as shall be advanced and paid into His Majesty's Treasury, in Manner therein mentioned, and towards the Discharge of the said Principal Sums; it was Enacted, That for all and every such Sum and Sums of Money, not exceeding in the Whole the Sum of One Hundred and Fifty Thousand Pounds, as should be actually paid by any Person or Persons into the Treasury, at the Instance of his Grace the Lord Lieutenant, or other Chief Governor or Governors of the Kingdom of Ireland, for the Time being, for the necessary Defence of this Kingdom, and for Discharging the several Sums of Money which had been, or should be Granted, during the said Session of Parliament, or which had been Granted, during the two Sessions of Parliament preceding the said last Session of Parliament, and remained unpaid, for making or continuing any Navigations, or other Publick Works in this Kingdom, there should be paid at the Receipt of the Exchequer, by the Hands of the Vice-Treasurer or Vice-Treasurers, or Paymaster-General, his or their Deputy or Deputies,

at

Georgii Tertii Regis.

CHAP. II.

at the End of every Six Kalendar Months from the respective Times of such Payments, to the Person or Persons so Paying or Lending the same, his, her, or their Executors, Administrators, or Assigns, an Interest, according to the Rate of Four Pounds per Centum, per Annum, without any Fee or Charge, and free from all Deductions, Defalcations, and Abatements whatsoever, until such Time as they should be respectively paid their Principal Money, at one intire Payment.

And Whereas subsequent to the passing the said Act, the Commons of Ireland, in Parliament assembled, in the said last Session, Resolved, That Whatever Sum or Sums of Money, not exceeding, in the Whole, the Sum of Three Hundred Thousand Pounds, should be paid into the Treasury, at the Instance of his Grace the Lord Lieutenant, or other Chief Governor or Governors of this Kingdom, for the Time being, to supply such Deficiency as might arise in the Aids Granted that Session of Parliament, for the Support of the Civil and Military Establishments, and other necessary Expences of Government, for the Defence of this Kingdom, for two Years, from the Twenty fifth Day of December, One thousand seven hundred and fifty nine,

should

should be made good by them, With an Interest for the same, at the Rate of Five Pounds for every Hundred Pounds, by the Year, to be computed from the respective Times such Sums should be advanced out of such Aids as should be Granted the next Session of Parliament; and further Resolved, That an Interest of One Pound for every Hundred Pounds, by the Year, should be made good by them, out of such Aids as should be Granted next Session of Parliament, to such Persons as had Advanced and Paid, or should Advance or Pay, any Sum or Sums of Money into the said Treasury, pursuant to the said Act of Parliament, over and above the Interest of Four Pounds for every Hundred Pounds, by the Year, already provided by the said Act.

And Whereas upon the Credit of the said Act of Parliament, and of the said Resolutions, not only the said Sum of One Hundred and Fifty Thousand Pounds, but also a considerable Part of the said Sum of Three Hundred Thousand Pounds, hath been paid by several Persons into the Treasury, at the Instance of his Grace the Lord Lieutenant, or other Chief Governor, or Governors of this Kingdom, and still remain unpaid:

We

Georgii Tertii Regis.

CHAP. II.

Be it Enacted by the King's Most Excellent Majesty, by and with the Advice and Consent of the Lords Spiritual and Temporal, and Commons in Parliament assembled, and by Authority of the same, That for all and every such Sum and Sums of Money, not Exceeding in the Whole the Sum of One Hundred and Fifty Thousand Pounds, as have been actually paid by any Person or Persons into the Treasury, pursuant to the said Act of Parliament, there shall be paid at the Receipt of His Majesty's Exchequer, by the Hands of the Vice-Treasurer, or Vice-Treasurers, his or their Deputy or Deputies, from the respective Times of such Payments, to the Person or Persons that so paid the same, his, her, or their Executors, Administrators, or Assigns, an Interest of One Pound for every Hundred Pounds by the Year, over and above the Interest of Four Pounds for every Hundred Pounds by the Year, already provided by the said Act, so as to make the Interest of such Sum and Sums Five Pounds a Year, for every Hundred Pounds, without any Fee or Charge, and free from all Deductions, Defalcations and Abatements Whatsoever, until such Time as they shall be respectively paid their principal Money at one intire Payment.

I And

CHAP. II. And be it further Enacted by the Authority aforesaid, That for all and every such Sum and Sums of Money, not exceeding in the Whole the Sum of Three Hundred Thousand Pounds, as have been, or shall be before the Twenty fifth Day of December, One thousand seven hundred and sixty one, actually paid by any Person or Persons into the Treasury, at the Instance of his Grace the Lord Lieutenant, or other Chief Governor or Governors of this Kingdom, for the Time being, to supply such Deficiency as may have arisen, or may Arise, in the Aids granted the last Session of Parliament for the Support of the Civil and Military Establishments, and other necessary Expences of Government, for the Defence of this Kingdom, there shall be paid at the Receipt of His Majesty's Exchequer, by the Hands of the Vice-Treasurer or Vice-Treasurers, or Pay-Master-General, his or their Deputy or Deputies, from the respective Times of such Payments, to the Person or Persons that have paid, or shall pay the same, his, her, or their Executors, Administrators, or Assigns, an Interest according to the Rate of Five Pounds a Year for every Hundred Pounds, without any Fee or Charge, and free from all Deductions, Defalcations,

Defalcations, and Abatements Whatsoever, until such Time as they shall be respectively paid their Principal Money, at One intire Payment.

And be it further Enacted by the Authority aforesaid, That Debentures, or Receipts, shall be given, and signed by the proper Officer of His Majesty's Treasury, for all and every Sum and Sums of Money, not exceeding in the Whole the Sum of Three Hundred Thousand Pounds, which have been, or shall be paid into the said Treasury, on Account of the said Sum of Three Hundred Thousand Pounds, payable at the said Treasury, to such Person or Persons, his, her, or their Executors, Administrators, or Assigns, as have paid, or shall pay in the same, with Interest, at the Rate of Five Pounds a Year, for every Hundred Pounds, and that any Person may by Indorsement on such Debenture, or Receipt, transfer the Right and Benefit of the Sum due on such Debenture or Receipt, which upon Notice to the Vice-Treasurer or Vice-Treasurers, his or their Deputy or Deputies, and an Entry or Memorial thereof made in the said Vice-Treasurer's Office (which the said Vice-Treasurer or Vice-Treasurers, his or their Deputy or Deputies, shall upon Request, without Charge, Fee, or Reward, make accordingly, and shall, on Request, permit the same to be viewed at the usual Office Hours, without Fee or Reward) shall intitle the Indorsee, or Assignee, his Executors, Administrators, or Assigns, to the sole Benefit of the Sum so transferred or assigned, and that the said Debenture or Receipt, may, in like Manner, be again assigned or transferred by such Assignee or Assignees, his, her, or their Executors or Administrators, and so from Time to Time, as often as Occasion may require; and that after such Assignment made, it shall not be in the Power of the Person or Persons who made such Assignment, to make Void, Release, or Discharge the said Assignment, or the Sum thereby transferred or assigned, or any Part thereof. And for securing the Repayment of such Sum or Sums of Money, not exceeding in the whole the said Sums of One Hundred and Fifty Thousand Pounds, and Three Hundred Thousand Pounds, as have been, or shall be so advanced and paid into the said Treasury, with Interest for the same, at the Rate of Five Pounds a Year, for every One Hundred Pounds; be it Enacted by the Authority aforesaid, That an additional Duty of Two Pounds per Tun, for and upon all Sorts of Wines of the Growth of Portugal, and of Four Pounds per Tun, for and upon all other Wines that

that shall be Imported into this Kingdom, from and after the Twenty fifth Day of December, One thousand seven hundred and sixty one, be Granted, Levied, Raised, and Paid to His Majesty, from the said Twenty fifth Day of December, One thousand seven hundred and sixty one, over and above the Hereditary Duties, and the several and respective Rates, Duties, and Impositions, that shall or may be granted to His Majesty in this Session of Parliament, and also an additional Duty of Forty Shillings per Pound Weight, for and upon all Velvets, and Manufactures made of, or mixed with Silk (except those of Great Britain, China, Persia, and the East Indies) that shall be Imported into this Kingdom, from and after the Twenty fifth Day of December, One thousand seven hundred and sixty one, be Levied, Raised, and Paid to His Majesty, from the said Twenty fifth Day of December, One thousand seven hundred and sixty one; and also an additional Duty of One Halfpenny per Pound Weight, for and upon all Hops that shall be Imported into this Kingdom, from and after the said Twenty fifth Day of December, One thousand seven hundred and sixty one; an additional Duty of Five Pounds per Centum, for and upon

K all

CHAP. II. all China, Earthen, Japanned, or Lacquered Ware, that shall be Imported into this Kingdom, from and after the said Twenty fifth Day of December, One thousand seven hundred and sixty one, as Valued and Rated for Custom by the Book of Rates; an additional Duty of Twenty Shillings per Tun, for and upon all Sorts of Vinegar that shall be Imported into this Kingdom, from and after the said Twenty Fifth Day of December, One thousand seven hundred and sixty one, be Levied, Raised, and Paid to His Majesty, His Heirs and Successors, from the said Twenty Fifth Day of December, One Thousand seven hundred and sixty one.

And be it further Enacted by the Authority aforesaid, That the said several Duties and Impositions, hereby Granted and Charged upon Wines, Velvets, and Manufactures made or mixed with Silk, the said Additional Duty of One Halfpenny per Pound Weight on Hops, the said Additional Duty of Five Pounds per Centum, on China, Earthen, Japanned, or Lacquered Ware, and the said Additional Duty of Twenty Shillings per Tun on Vinegar, be Raised, Collected, Levied, and Paid to His Majesty, His Heirs, and Successors, from the said Twenty fifth Day of December,

cember, One thousand seven hundred and sixty one, until the Twenty fifth Day of March, which will be in the Year of Our Lord, One thousand seven hundred and sixty two, inclusive, and no longer, over and above all other Duties, that shall be then payable for the same, by Virtue of any Act of Parliament that shall be then in Force in this Kingdom.

And be it further Enacted by the Authority aforesaid, That if the said Wines, or other Merchandizes herein before mentioned, upon which the said Additional and other Duties are hereby charged, shall be again Exported by any Merchant or Merchants, that is or are a Subject or Subjects of this Realm, or any other His Majesty's Dominions, within Eighteen Months, or by Merchants Strangers, within Twelve Months, after the Importation thereof, and that due Proof be first made, by Certificate, from the proper Officers, of the due Entry and Payment of the said Additional and other Duties hereby Granted, and that all other Requisites shall be performed, which are by Law required to be performed in those Cases, where the Duties of Excise are to be repaid, that then the said Additional and other Duties, shall, without any Delay or Re-

CHAP. II. ward, be Repaid or Allowed, unto such Merchant or Merchants so Exporting the same, Within one Month after Demand thereof, or the Security for the said Additional and other Duties, by this Act charged, shall be vacated, as to so much as shall be so Exported; any Thing herein contained to the contrary notwithstanding.

And be it further Enacted by the Authority aforesaid, That all and every the several and respective Additional and other Duties hereby Granted, shall be Raised, Answered, Collected, and Paid unto His Majesty, His Heirs and Successors, during the Time aforesaid, at the same Time, and in like Manner, and by such Ways, Means, and Methods, and by such Rules and Directions, and under such Penalties and Forfeitures, and with such Powers, as are appointed, directed, and expressed, in and by an Act made in this Kingdom, in the Fourteenth and Fifteenth Years of the Reign of King Charles the Second, Intitled, An Act for the Settling the Excise or New Impost upon His Majesty, His Heirs, and Successors, according to the Book of Rates therein inserted; or by any other Law now in Force, relating to the Revenue of Excise in this Kingdom, as fully and effectually, to all Intents and Purposes, as

if

if the same were particularly mentioned, specified, and Enacted again in the Body of this present Act, with like Remedy of Appeal, to and for the Party grieved, as in and by the said Act of Excise, or any other Law or Laws now in being, relating to the Duties of Excise, is provided.

And be it further Enacted by the Authority aforesaid, That neither the Sixpence per Pound, nor any other Fee, shall be payable to, or be deducted or received by the Vice-Treasurer or Vice-Treasurers, Receiver, or Pay-Master-General, Clerk of the Pells, or any other Officer or Officers of this Kingdom, for, or on Account of, or out of the Aids hereby granted to His Majesty, or of any Payment to be made thereout, in pursuance of this Act.

And be it further Enacted by the Authority aforesaid, That the said several Duties and Aids hereby granted to His Majesty, shall be applied by the Vice-Treasurer or Vice-Treasurers, his or their Deputy or Deputies, to pay an Interest, at the Rate of Five Pounds per Centum, per Annum, in Lieu of the said Interest of Four Pounds per Centum, per Annum, provided by the said Act of the last Session of Parliament, for all

Chap. II. all such Sum and Sums of Money, not exceeding, in the Whole, the Sum of One Hundred and Fifty Thousand Pounds, as have been advanced and paid into the said Treasury, in Pursuance of the said last mentioned Act, and also an Interest, at the Rate of Five Pounds per Centum, per Annum, for all such Sum and Sums of Money, not exceeding in the Whole the Sum of Three Hundred Thousand Pounds, as have been, or shall be advanced and paid into the said Treasury, in Pursuance of the said Resolution of the said Commons, and towards the Discharge of such Principal Sum and Sums.

And be it further Enacted by the Authority aforesaid, that if any Part of the said Principal Sums shall remain Due and unpaid, on the Twenty fifth Day of March, which shall be in the Year of Our Lord, One thousand seven hundred and sixty two, the same shall be well and truly satisfied and paid unto the several Persons, their Executors, Administrators, and Assigns, respectively, to Whom the same shall be then Due, together with such Interest for the same, as shall be then Due, at the Rate of Five Pounds per Centum, per Annum, Without any Deduction, Defalcation, or Abatement Whatsoever.

And

CHAP. II.

And be it further Enacted by the Authority aforesaid, That from and after the said Twenty fifth Day of December, One thousand seven hundred and sixty one, a seperate and distinct Account shall be kept by the Proper Officers, of the Duties and Aids granted by this Act, or any other Act of Parliament now in Force in this Kingdom, and appropriated to Particular Uses, and that the Commissioners of His Majesty's Revenue in their Abstracts, shall return an Account of the several Duties and Taxes so appropriated, and that every Collector, or Receiver of the said Duties and Taxes, do take a seperate Receipt for the same, when paid into His Majesty's Treasury, which said Receipt, the Vice-Treasurer, or Vice-Treasurers, his or their Deputy or Deputies, is, and are required to give accordingly.

CHAP. III.

AN ACT

TO

Perpetuate, with Amendments, a Clause in an Act passed in the Ninth Year of His late Majesty King *George* the Second, Intitled, *An Act for the more effectual Assigning of Judgments, and for the more speedy Recovery of Rents by Distress.*

DUBLIN:

Printed by BOULTER GRIERSON, Printer to the King's Most Excellent Majesty. MDCCLXII.

AN ACT TO

Perpetuate, with Amendments, a Clause in an Act passed in the Ninth Year of His late Majesty King *George* the Second, Intitled, *An Act for the more effectual Assigning of Judgments, and for the more speedy Recovery of Rents by Distress.*

CHAP. III.

WHEREAS by an Act of Parliament passed in this Kingdom, in the Ninth Year of His late Majesty King George the Second, Intitled,

CHAP. III. An Act for the more effectual Assigning of Judgments, and for the more speedy Recovery of Rents by Distress; it has, for the Reasons therein mentioned, Enacted (among other Things) That in all Cases, the Recital of a Lease for a Year, in the Deed of Release, shall be deemed, and taken to be, full and sufficient Evidence of such Lease, which Act being Temporary, hath been continued by subsequent Acts passed in this Kingdom.

And Whereas the said recited Clause hath been found, by Experience, to be useful and fit to be made a perpetual Law; Be it therefore Enacted by the King's Most Excellent Majesty, by and with the Advice and Consent of the Lords Spiritual and Temporal, and Commons in Parliament assembled, and by the Authority of the same, That the said recited Act passed in the Ninth Year of His late Majesty, so far forth as the same relates to the making the Recital of a Lease for a Year, in the Deed of Release, Evidence of such Lease, shall be and remain in full Force, to all Intents and Purposes, for ever.

And

CHAP. III.

And be it further Enacted and Declared by the Authority aforesaid, That in all Cases of Pleading Deeds of Lease and Release, wherein it may be necessary to alledge the bringing such Deeds into Court, it shall be sufficient to alledge the bringing into Court the Deed of Release, in which the Recital of such Lease shall, to all purposes whatsoever, be as effectual as producing the same.

CHAP. IV.

AN ACT

FOR

Allowing further Time to Persons in Offices or Employments, to Qualify themselves, pursuant to an Act, Intitled, *An Act to Prevent the further Growth of Popery.*

DUBLIN:
Printed by BOULTER GRIERSON, Printer to the King's Most Excellent Majesty. MDCCLXII.

AN ACT FOR

Allowing further Time to Persons in Offices or Employments, to Qualify themselves, pursuant to an Act, intitled, *An Act to prevent the further Growth of Popery.*

CHAP. IV.

WHEREAS several Persons Well Affected to His Majesty's Government, and the Church of Ireland, as by Law Established, may have through Ignorance neglected, or been prevented by Sickness, or other Unavoidable Causes, from taking and subscribing the Oaths, and making and subscribing the Declaration, and from Receiving the Sacrament of the Lord's Supper, according to to the Directions of an Act made in this Kingdom, in the Second Year of the Reign of Her late Majesty Queen Anne, Intitled, An Act to prevent the further Growth of Popery; and by their Inadvertency may have incurred great Penalties; Be it Enacted by the King's Most Excellent Majesty, by and with the Advice and Consent of the Lords Spiritual and Temporal, and Commons in Parliament Assembled, and by the Authority of the same, That all and every Person or Persons who have incurred any Penalties and Incapacities in the said Act, Intitled, An Act to prevent the further Growth of Popery, mentioned, by neglecting to Qualify themselves according to the said Act, shall be, and are hereby Indemnified, Freed, and Discharged of and from all Incapacities, Disabilities, Forfeitures, and Penalties incurred, by Reason of such Omission or Neglect, as aforesaid, and that no Act or Acts done by them, or any of them, or by Authority derived from them, or any of them, and not yet avoided, shall be questioned or avoided, by Reason of such Neglect or Omission, but all such Acts shall be, and are hereby Declared and Enacted to be, as Good and Effectual, as if all and every such Person and Persons had taken and subscribed the

said

said Oaths, and Received the said Sacrament, and made and subscribed the said Declaration in Manner as aforesaid; any Thing in the said Act to the Contrary notwithstanding.

Provided such Person or Persons do and shall take and subscribe the said Oaths, and receive the said Sacrament, and make, repeat, and subscribe the said Declaration, in such Manner and Form, and in such Place and Places as are directed and appointed by the said Act to prevent the further Growth of Popery, on or before the First Day of August, which shall be in the Year of Our Lord, One thousand seven hundred and sixty two.

Provided always, That this Act, or any Thing herein contained, shall not extend to Restore or Intitle any Person or Persons to any Office or Employment, already actually avoided by Judgment of any of His Majesty's Courts of Record, or already filled up by any other Person, but that such Office or Employment shall be and remain in the Person or Persons, who is or are now Intitled by Law to the same, as if this Act had never been made.

CHAP. V.

AN ACT

FOR

Granting to His Majesty, the several Duties, Rates, and Impositions, therein expressed, to be applied to pay an Interest, at the Rate of Five Pounds *per Centum, per Annum*, for the several Sums therein provided for, and towards the Discharge of the said Principal Sums.

DUBLIN:

Printed by BOULTER GRIERSON, Printer to the King's Most Excellent Majesty. MDCCLXII.

AN ACT

FOR

Granting to His Majesty, the several Duties, Rates, and Impositions, therein expressed, to be applied to pay an Interest, at the Rate of Five Pounds *per Centum, per Annum*, for the several Sums therein provided for, and towards the Discharge of the said Principal Sums.

CHAP. V.

WHEREAS by an Act passed in the last Session of Parliament, Intituled, An Act for Granting to His Majesty, a further Additional Duty on Wine, Silk,

CHAP. V.

Silk, Hops, *China*, Earthen, Japanned, and Lacquered Ware, and Vinegar, to be applied to pay an Interest of Four Pounds *per Centum, per Annum*, for such Sums of Money, not exceeding in the Whole, the Sum of One Hundred and Fifty Thousand Pounds, as shall be advanced and paid into His Majesty's Treasury, in Manner therein mentioned, and towards the Discharge of the said Principal Sums; It was Enacted, That for all and every such Sum and Sums of Money, not exceeding in the Whole the Sum of One Hundred and Fifty Thousand Pounds, as should be actually paid by any Person or Persons into the Treasury, at the Instance of his Grace the Lord Lieutenant, or other Chief Governor or Governors of the Kingdom of Ireland, for the Time being, for the necessary Defence of this Kingdom, and for Discharging the several Sums of Money which had been, or should be Granted, during the said Session of Parliament, or which had been Granted, during the two Sessions of Parliament next preceding the said last Session of Parliament, and remained unpaid, for making or continuing any Navigations, or other Publick Works in this Kingdom, there should be paid at the Receipt of the Exchequer, by the Hands of the Vice-Treasurer or Vice-Treasurers, or Paymaster-General, his or their Deputy or Deputies,

at

CHAP. V.

at the End of every Six Kalendar Months from the respective Times of such Payments, to the Person or Persons so paying or Lending the same, his, her, or their Executors, Administrators, or Assigns, an Interest, according to the Rate of Four Pounds per Centum per Annum, without any Fee or Charge, and free from all Deductions, Defalcations, and Abatements whatsoever, until such Time as they should be respectively paid their Principal Money, at one intire Payment.

And Whereas, subsequent to the passing the said Act, the Commons of Ireland, in Parliament Assembled, in the said last Session, Resolved, That whatever Sum or Sums of Money, not exceeding in the Whole, the Sum of Three Hundred Thousand Pounds, should be paid into the Treasury, at the Instance of His Grace the Lord Lieutenant, or other Chief Governor or Governors of this Kingdom, for the Time being, to supply such Deficiencies as might arise in the Aids granted that Session of Parliament, for the Support of the Civil and Military Establishments, and other necessary Expences of Government, for the Defence of this Kingdom, for Two Years, from the Twenty Fifth Day of December, One thousand seven hundred and fifty nine, should be made good by them, with an Interest

CHAP. V.

terest for the same, at the Rate of Five Pounds for every One Hundred by the Year, to be computed from the respective Times, such Sums should be Advanced, out of such Aids as should be Granted the next Session of Parliament; and further Resolved, That an Interest of One Pound, for every One Hundred Pounds by the Year, should be made good by them, out of such Aids as should be Granted next Session of Parliament, to such Persons as had Advanced and Paid, or should Advance or Pay, any Sum or Sums of Money into the said Treasury, pursuant to the said Act of Parliament, over and above the Interest of Four Pounds for every One Hundred Pounds by the Year, already Provided by the said Act.

And whereas by an Act passed in this Session of Parliament, Intituled, An Act for Granting to His Majesty a further Additional Duty on Wine, Silk, Hops, *China*, Earthen, Japanned, Lacquered Ware, and Vinegar, and for better Securing the Repayment of One Hundred and Fifty Thousand Pounds, paid into the Treasury for the Support of His Majesty's Government, pursuant to an Act of the last Session, together with the Interest thereof, and for Securing the Repayment of such Sums of Money, not exceeding in the Whole the Sum of Three Hundred Thousand Pounds, as have been or shall

shall be paid into the Treasury, or shall be advanced to His present Majesty, pursuant to the Resolutions of the House of Commons, the last Session of Parliament, together with the Interest thereof, It Was (among other things) Enacted, That for all and every such Sum and Sums of Money, not exceeding in the Whole the Sum of One Hundred and Fifty Thousand Pounds, as had been actually paid by any Person or Persons into the Treasury, pursuant to the said Act of Parliament of the last Session, there should be paid at the Receipt of Your Majesty's Exchequer, by the Hands of the Vice-Treasurer, or Vice-Treasurers, his or their Deputy or Deputies, from the respective Times of such Payments, to the Person or Persons that so paid the same, his, her, or their Executors, Administrators, or Assigns, an Interest of One Pound for every One Hundred Pounds by the Year, over and above the Interest of Four Pounds for every One Hundred Pounds by the Year, already provided by the said Act of the last Session, so as to make the Interest of such Sum and Sums Five Pounds a Year, for every One Hundred Pounds, without any Fee or Charge, and free from all Deductions, Defalcations, and Abatements Whatsoever, until such Time as they should be respectively paid their Principal Money at one intire Payment: And it Was further Enacted,

CHAP. V.

CHAP. V.

Enacted, that for all and every such Sum and Sums of Money, not exceeding in the Whole the Sum of Three Hundred Thousand Pounds, as had been, or should be, before the Twenty fifth Day of December, One thousand seven hundred and sixty one, actually paid by any Person or Persons into the Treasury, at the Instance of his Grace the Lord Lieutenant, or other Chief Governor or Governors of this Kingdom, for the Time being, to supply such Deficiency as may have arisen, or might arise, in the Aids granted last Session of Parliament, for the Support of the Civil and Military Establishments, and other necessary Expences of Government, for the Defence of this Kingdom, there should be paid, at the Receipt of Your Majesty's Exchequer, by the Hands of the Vice-Treasurer, or Vice-Treasurers, or Pay-Master-General, his or their Deputy or Deputies, from the respective Times of such Payments, to the Person or Persons that have paid, or should pay the same, his, her, or their Executors, Administrators, or Assigns, an Interest, according to the Rate of Five Pounds a Year for every One Hundred Pounds, without any Fee or Charge, and free from all Deductions, Defalcations and Abatements whatsoever, until such Time as they should be respectively paid their Principal Money at one intire Payment.

And

CHAP. V.

And whereas upon the Credit of the said Act of Parliament of the last Session, and of the said Resolutions of the House of Commons, not only the said Sum of One hundred and fifty thousand Pounds, but also the Sum of Two hundred thousand Pounds, Part of the said Sum of Three hundred thousand Pounds, hath been paid by several Persons into Your Majesty's Treasury, which said Sum of One hundred and fifty thousand Pounds, and Two hundred thousand Pounds, amount in the Whole to the Sum of Three hundred and fifty thousand Pounds.

And whereas the said Sum of Three hundred and fifty thousand Pounds remains still unpaid, and it may be necessary that a further Sum or Sums of Money should be borrowed to supply such Deficiencies as may arise in the Aids granted this Session of Parliament, for the Support of Your Majesty's Government:

We therefore, Your Majesty's most Dutiful and Loyal Subjects, the Commons of Ireland, in Parliament assembled, do most humbly beseech Your Majesty, that it may be Enacted, and be it Enacted by the King's Most Excellent Majesty, by and with the Advice and Consent of the Lords Spiritual

CHAP. V.

tual and Temporal, and Commons in this present Parliament assembled, and by the Authority of the same, That a further additional Duty of Six Pounds per Tun, for and upon all Sorts of Wine of the Growth of France or Spain, and Three Pounds per Tun, for and upon all Sorts of Wine of the Growth of Portugal, and of Five Pounds per Tun, for and upon all other Wines that shall be imported into this Kingdom, from and after the Twenty fifth Day of March, One thousand seven hundred and sixty two; and also an additional Duty of Forty Shillings per Pound Weight, for and upon all Velvets and Manufactures, made of, or mixed with Silk (except those of Great Britain, China, Persia, and the East-Indies) that shall be Imported into this Kingdom, from and after the Twenty fifth Day of March, One thousand seven hundred and sixty two, be Granted, Raised, Levied, and Paid to Your Majesty, from the said Twenty fifth Day of March, One thousand seven hundred and sixty two; an additional Duty of One Half penny per Pound Weight, for and upon all Hops that shall be Imported into this Kingdom, from and after the Twenty fifth Day of March, One thousand seven hundred and sixty two; an additional Duty of Five Pounds per Centum, for and upon all China, Earthen, Japanned, or Lacquered Ware, as valued or rated for

Custom

Custom by the Book of Rates, that shall be Imported into this Kingdom, from and after the said Twenty fifth Day of March, One thousand seven hundred and sixty two; an additional Duty of Thirty Shillings per Tun, for and upon all Sorts of Vinegar that shall be Imported into this Kingdom, from and after the said Twenty fifth Day of March, One thousand seven hundred and sixty two; a further additional Duty of Two Pence per Gallon, for and upon every Gallon of Aqua Vitæ, Strong Waters, and Spirits, that shall be made or distilled within this Kingdom for Sale, to be paid by the first Maker or Distiller thereof, from and after the said Twenty fifth Day of March, One thousand seven hundred and sixty two; a further additional Duty of Two Pence per Pound, for and upon all Coffee that shall be Imported into this Kingdom, from and after the Twenty fifth Day of March, One thousand seven hundred and sixty two; a Duty of Ten Shillings, to be paid by every Person that doth or shall sell, or tap out by Retail, any Cyder, at any Time between the said Twenty fifth Day of March, One thousand seven hundred and sixty two, and the Twenty fifth Day of March, One thousand seven hundred and sixty three inclusive; and a Duty of seven Shillings and Six Pence (being at the Rate of Ten Shillings by

Chap. V.

the Year) to be paid by every Person that doth or shall sell, or tap out Cyder by Retail, at any Time between the said Twenty-fifth Day of March, One thousand seven hundred and sixty three, and the Twenty-fifth Day of December, One thousand seven hundred and sixty three, inclusive; a Duty of One Penny per Gallon, for and upon all Cyder that shall be Sold, or tapped out by Retail, to be paid by the Person who shall sell or tap out the same by Retail, from and after the said Twenty-fifth Day of March, One thousand seven hundred and sixty two; an additional Duty of Twenty Shillings, to be paid by every Person for every Coach, Chariot, Berlin, Calash, or Chaise, with four Wheels, which such Person shall keep in his or her Possession (except Hackney, or Stage-Coaches, and Coaches kept by Coach-Makers for Sale) at any Time between the said Twenty-fifth Day of March, One thousand seven hundred and sixty two, and the Twenty-fifth Day of March, One thousand seven hundred and sixty three, inclusive; and a Duty of Fifteen Shillings (being at the Rate of Twenty Shillings by the Year) to be paid by every Person for every Coach, Chariot, Berlin, Calash, or Chaise with four Wheels, which such Person shall keep in his or her Possession (except as aforesaid) between the said Twenty-fifth

Day

Day of March, One thousand seven hundred and sixty-three, and the Twenty fifth Day of December, One thousand seven hundred and sixty three, inclusive; an additional Duty of Six Pence per Tun, for and upon every Tun of Soap-Boilers Waste, and so in Proportion for a greater or lesser Quantity, that shall be exported out of this Kingdom to Parts beyond the Seas, from and after the Twenty-fifth Day of March, One thousand seven hundred and sixty two, be granted, raised, levied, and paid to Your Majesty, Your Heirs, and Successors, from the said Twenty-fifth Day of March, One thousand seven hundred and sixty two.

And be it further Enacted by the Authority aforesaid, That the said several additional Duties and Impositions hereby granted and charged, for and upon Wines, Velvets, and Manufactures made of, or mixed with Silk; the said additional Duty of One Half Penny per Pound Weight on Hops; the said additional Duty of Five Pounds, per Centum, on China, Earthen, Japanned, and Lacquered Ware; the said additional Duty of Thirty Shillings per Tun on Vinegar; the said further additional Duty of Two Pence per Gallon on Aqua Vitæ, Strong Waters, and Spirits; the said further additional Duty of Two Pence per Pound, for and upon all Coffee; the said respective

Duties

CHAP. V.

Duties of Ten Shillings, and Seven Shillings and Six Pence, to be paid by every Person that doth or shall sell Cyder by Retail; the said Duty of One Penny per Gallon, for and upon all Cyder that shall be sold or tapped out by Retail; the said respective additional Duties of Twenty Shillings, and Fifteen Shillings, on every Coach, Chariot, Berlin, Calash, or Chaise with four Wheels; and the said Duty of Six Pence per Tun on Soap-Boilers Waste, be granted, raised, levied, Collected, and paid to Your Majesty, Your Heirs and Successors, from the said Twenty fifth Day of March, One thousand seven hundred and sixty two, until the Twenty fifth Day of December, which will be in the Year of our Lord, One thousand seven hundred and sixty three, inclusive, and no longer, over and above all other Duties payable for the same, by Virtue of any Act of Parliament now in Force in this Kingdom.

And be it further Enacted by the Authority aforesaid, That if the said Wines, and other Merchandizes herein before mentioned, upon which the said additional Duties are hereby charged, upon the Importation thereof, shall be again exported by any Merchant or Merchants, that is or are a Subject or Subjects of this Realm, or any other his Majesty's Dominions, within Twenty four

four Kalendar Months, or by Merchant Strangers, within Twelve Kalendar Months after the Importation thereof, and that due Proof be first made by Certificate, from the proper Officers, of the due Entry and Payment of the said additional Duties hereby granted, and that all other Requisites shall be performed, which are by Law required to be performed in those Cases, where the Duties of Excise are to be repaid; that then, the said additional Duties hereby imposed, shall, without any Delay or Reward, be repaid, or allowed unto such Merchant or Merchants so exporting the same, within one Month after Demand thereof, or the Security for the said additional Duties, by this Act charged, shall be vacated, as to so much as shall be so exported; any Thing herein contained to the contrary notwithstanding.

And be it further Enacted by the Authority aforesaid, That from and after the Twenty fourth Day of June, One thousand seven hundred and sixty two, no Person or Persons whatsoever shall sell, or tap out by Retail, any Cyder within this Kingdom, but only such as shall be licenced according to the Directions of this Act, under such Penalty as herein after is expressed.

CHAP. V.

And be it further Enacted by the Authority aforesaid, That from and after the Twenty fifth Day of March, One thousand seven hundred and sixty two, it shall and may be lawful to and for the Chief Commissioners of His Majesty's Excise, or any Three of them, and the Collectors of His Majesty's Excise, in their several and respective Districts, from Time to Time, to issue and grant such Licences, for the selling and tapping out Cyder by Retail; and that for every such Licence, so to be granted, the Sum of One Shilling and One Penny, and no more, shall be paid, or demanded, as a Fee for the same. And if any Person or Persons shall, from and after the Twenty fourth Day of June, One thousand seven hundred and sixty two, sell, or tap out Cyder by Retail, without such Licence as aforesaid, every such Person so offending, shall, for every Time he or she shall so offend, forfeit and pay the Sum of Five Pounds.

And for the better ordering and collecting the said Duty of One Penny per Gallon, for and upon all Cyder that shall be sold, or tapped out by Retail; Be it further Enacted by the Authority aforesaid, That it shall and may be lawful to and for the Gauger or Gaugers, and Officers of Excise,

within

Chap. V.

within their respective Districts, from Time to Time, from and after the said Twenty-fifth Day of March, One thousand seven hundred and sixty two, to enter, in the Day-time, into the Houses, Out-Houses, Store-Houses, and Cellars, of every Retailer or Retailers of Cyder, and to take an Account of all such Cyder as shall be found in the Possession of such Retailer or Retailers of Cyder, and to charge such Retailer and Retailers with the said Duty of One Penny per Gallon accordingly.

And be it further Enacted by the Authority aforesaid, That from and after the said Twenty-fifth Day of March, One thousand seven hundred and sixty two, every Retailer of Cyder, shall shew to the Gauger, or Officers of Excise, on Demand, all his or her Stock of Cyder then on Hand: And in Case any such Retailer or Retailers of Cyder, or his, her, or their Servant or Servants (in Case such Retailer or Retailers shall not be present When the Gauger, or Officers of Excise, shall come to such Retailer's House to take Stock, as aforesaid) shall refuse to make Declaration, and shew all his or her Stock of Cyder then on Hand, every such Retailer shall, for every such Offence, forfeit and lose the Sum of Ten Pounds. And if such Gauger or Officers of Excise, shall, after Declaration made

Chap.
V.
made as aforesaid, find any Cyder in the possession or Custody of such Retailer or Retailers, over and above the Quantity so shewn and declared, such Retailer shall likewise forfeit and lose the Sum of Ten Pounds.

And for the better Collecting the said Duty, chargeable on every Person who shall keep any Carriages with four Wheels (except as before excepted) Be it Enacted by the Authority aforesaid, That every Person, who from and after the Twenty-fifth Day of March, One thousand seven hundred and sixty two, shall have or keep any Coach, Chariot, Berlin, Calash, or Chaise with four Wheels, shall, within three Kalendar Months after the said Twenty-fifth Day of March, or within three Kalendar Months after he or she shall have, or keep any such Coach, Chariot, Berlin, Calash, or Chaise with four Wheels, by Writing under his or her Hand, certify to the Collector of the District where he or she shall reside or dwell, a true Account of every such Coach, Chariot, Berlin, Calash, and Chaise with four Wheels, which he or she shall have or keep (except Hackney or Stage-Coaches, and Coaches kept by Coach-Makers for Sale) with the Name of the Place, and Parish, of his or her usual Residence or Abode, which said Certificates shall be kept by the respective

spective Collectors of the several Districts in this Kingdom, now, or hereafter to be appointed by the Commissioners of His Majesty's Revenue in this Kingdom, or any Three or more of them, and shall be also entered in a Book, to be by them respectively kept for that Purpose, and a Number shall be entered on each Certificate, registered; and that the said Collectors respectively, shall, under their Hands, on or before the Twenty fifth Day of December in every Year, give a true List of all Coaches, Chariots, Berlins, Calashes, and Chaises with four Wheels, from Time to Time, returned to them respectively, in such Certificates, with the Names of the Persons, and Places of their Abode, respectively mentioned in such respective Certificates, to the Person, who for the Time being, shall be appointed by the Commissioners of His Majesty's Revenue of Excise, or any Three of them, to collect and receive the said Duties; and that such Person and Persons as shall be appointed by the said Commissioners of Excise, or any Three of them, to collect the said Duties on Coaches, Chariots, Berlins, Calashes, and Chaises with four Wheels, shall have full Power and Authority to collect and receive the same, and shall respectively sign and deliver Acquittances without Fee or Reward for the same, and shall keep Duplicates thereof, in a Book to be kept for

T 2   that

CHAP.
V.

that Purpose, in the same Manner as Acquittances are given and kept for the Duty on Fire-Hearths, and shall respectively return the Book, containing the Duplicates of such Acquittances, to such Person and Persons, and at the same Times, and to be disposed of in the same Manner, as Books containing the Duplicates of Acquittances for the said Duty on Fire-Hearths are returned.

And be it further Enacted by the Authority aforesaid, That if any Person or Persons shall have, or keep any Coach, Chariot, Berlin, Calash, or Chaise with four Wheels, chargeable with the said Duty, by Virtue of this Act, which shall not be certified in Manner as aforesaid, then, and in such Case, every such Person and Persons, so having or keeping such Coach, Chariot, Berlin, Calash, or Chaise with four Wheels, not certified as aforesaid, shall, for such Neglect, forfeit the Sum of Five Pounds; Provided nevertheless, that every Person (except as before excepted) having in his or her Keeping or Possession any Coach, Chariot, Berlin, Calash, or Chaise with four Wheels, belonging to another, shall be charged for every such Coach, Chariot, Berlin, Calash, or Chaise with four Wheels, with the said Duty imposed by this Act, in the same manner as the

Owner,

Owner, or Proprietor thereof, is, or ought to be charged, or chargeable for the same by this Act.

And be it further Enacted by the Authority aforesaid, That the Person or Persons who, for the Time being, shall be authorized and impowered to collect and levy the said Duty on Coaches, Chariots, Berlins, Calashes, and Chaises with four Wheels, shall pay the same to the said Collectors of the several Districts, where the said Duties shall be collected and raised, and that the said Collectors shall keep separate and distinct Accounts thereof, and pay the same into His Majesty's Treasury, as other Money received by them for the Use of His Majesty.

And be it further Enacted by the Authority aforesaid, That all and every the several and respective additional and other Duties, hereby granted, shall be raised, answered, collected, and paid unto Your Majesty, Your Heirs, and Successors, during the Term aforesaid, at the same Time, and in like Manner, and by such Ways, Means, and Methods, and by such Rules and Directions, and under such Penalties and Forfeitures (except wherein it is by this present Act otherwise directed) and with such Powers as are appointed,

CHAP. V.

pointed, directed, and expressed, in and by an Act made in this Kingdom, in the Fourteenth and Fifteenth Years of the Reign of King Charles the Second, Intituled, An Act for the Settling of the Excise, or New Impost, upon His Majesty, His Heirs and Successors, according to the Book of Rates therein inserted; or by any other Law now in Force, relative to the Revenue of Excise in this Kingdom, as fully and effectually, to all Intents and Purposes, as if the same were particularly mentioned, specified, and enacted again in the Body of this present Act, with like Remedy of Appeal, to and for the Party grieved, as in and by the said Acts of Excise, or any other Law or Laws now in being, relating to the Duties of Excise, is provided.

And be it further Enacted by the Authority aforesaid, That neither the Six Pence per Pound, nor any other Fee, shall be payable to, or be deducted or received by the Vice-Treasurer, or Vice-Treasurers, Receiver, or Pay-Master-General, Clerk of the Pells, or any other Officer or Officers of this Kingdom, for or on Account of, or out of the Aids hereby granted to Your Majesty, or of any Payment to be made thereout, in pursuance of this Act.

And

And be it further Enacted by the Authority aforesaid, That all and every the several and respective additional and other Duties, hereby granted to Your Majesty, shall be applied to pay an Interest, at the Rate of Five Pounds per Centum per Annum, for the said Sum of Three Hundred and Fifty Thousand Pounds already borrowed, and now remaining unpaid; and also the like Interest for such further Sum or Sums of Money, not exceeding in the Whole, the Sum of Four Hundred Thousand Pounds Sterling, as shall be actually paid into Your Majesty's Treasury, at the Instance of His Excellency the Lord Lieutenant, or other Chief Governor or Governors of this Kingdom, for the Time being, to supply such Deficiencies as may arise in the Aids granted this Session of Parliament, for the Support of Your Majesty's Civil and Military Establishments, and other necessary Expences of Government, and towards the Discharge of such Principal Sum and Sums, as have been already borrowed, and of such Sum and Sums as shall be borrowed, for the Purpose aforesaid.

CHAP. V.

And be it further Enacted by the Authority aforesaid, That the several Debentures and Receipts, which have heretofore been made

CHAP. V. made out, and given for the Payment of the said Sum of Three Hundred and Fifty Thousand Pounds, already borrowed, shall be called in and cancelled, as soon as conveniently may be done, after the Twenty-fifth Day of March, One thousand seven hundred and sixty-two, by the Vice-Treasurer, or Vice-Treasurers, his or their Deputy or Deputies; and that all Interest that shall be due thereon on the said Twenty-fifth Day of March, One thousand seven hundred and sixty-two, shall be paid to the Person or Persons respectively intitled to the same; and that the said Vice-Treasurer or Vice-Treasurers, his or their Deputy or Deputies, shall make out and deliver new Debentures to such Person or Persons respectively, their Executors, Administrators, or Assigns, as are or shall be intitled to the said Debentures so called in, for the Principal Sums contained in such Debentures; and that there shall be paid an Interest for the same, from the said Twenty-fifth Day of March, One thousand seven hundred and sixty-two, at the End of every Six Calendar Months, at the Rate of Five Pounds per Centum per Annum, without any Fee or Charge, and free from all Deductions, Defalcations, and Abatements whatsoever, until such

such Time as they shall be paid their Principal Money at one intire Payment.

CHAP. V.

And be it further Enacted by the Authority aforesaid, That for all and every such further Sum and Sums of Money, not exceeding in the Whole the Sum of Four Hundred Thousand Pounds, as shall be actually paid by any Person or Persons into Your Majesty's Treasury, to supply such Deficiencies as may arise in the Aids granted this Session of Parliament, for the Support of Your Majesty's Civil and Military Establishments, and other necessary Expences of Government, there shall be paid, at the Receipt of Your Majesty's Exchequer, by the Hands of the Vice-Treasurer or Vice-Treasurers, his or their Deputy or Deputies, at the End of every Six Calendar Months, to be computed from the respective Times of such Payments, to the Person or Persons so paying or lending the same, his, her, or their Executors, Administrators, or Assigns, an Interest, at the Rate of Five Pounds per Centum per Annum, without any Fee or Charge, and free from all Defalcations, Deductions, or Abatements whatsoever, until such Time as they shall be respectively paid their Principal Money, at one intire Payment.

F

And

CHAP.
V. And be it further Enacted by the Authority aforesaid, That Debentures shall be given, and signed by the proper Officers of Your Majesty's Treasury, for all and every Sum and Sums of Money, not exceeding in the Whole the said Sum of Four Hundred Thousand Pounds, which shall be paid into the Receipt of Your Majesty's Exchequer, on Account of the said intended Loan, payable at Your Majesty's Treasury, to such Person or Persons, his, her, or their Executors, Administrators, or Assigns, as shall subscribe and pay in the same, with Interest, at the Rate of Five Pounds per Centum per Annum.

And be it further Enacted by the Authority aforesaid, That all and every the said Debentures shall be assignable, and that any Person or Persons, to whom such Debenture or Debentures shall be made out and given, may, by Indorsement on such Debenture or Debentures, transfer the Right and Benefit of the Sum due on such Debenture or Debentures, Which, upon Notice to the Vice-Treasurer or Vice-Treasurers, his or their Deputy or Deputies, and an Entry or Memorial thereof made in the said Vice-Treasurer's Office, Which the said Vice-Treasurer or Vice-Treasurers, his or their Deputy or Deputies,

CHAP. V.

ties, shall, upon Request, without Charge, Fee, or Reward, make accordingly, and shall, on Request, permit the same to be viewed at the usual Office-Hours, without Fee or Reward, shall intitle the Indorsee or Assignee, his Executors, Administrators, or Assigns, to the sole Benefit of the Sum so transferred or assigned, and that the said Debenture or Debentures may, in like Manner, be again assigned or transferred, by such Assignee or Assignees, his, her, or their Executors or Administrators, and so from Time to Time, as often as Occasion may require; and that after such Assignment made, it shall not be in the Power of the Person or Persons who made such Assignment, to make void, release, or discharge the said Assignment, or the Sum thereby transferred or assigned, or any Part thereof.

And be it further Enacted by the Authority aforesaid, That if any Part of the said Principal Sums, which have been, or shall be so advanced and paid into Your Majesty's Treasury, as aforesaid, shall remain due and unpaid, on the Twenty-fifth Day of December, which shall be in the Year of Our Lord, One thousand seven hundred and sixty-three, the same shall be well and truly satisfied and paid unto the several Persons, their Executors, Administrators,

Chap. V. trators, and Assigns respectively, to whom the same shall be then due, together with such Interest for the same, as shall be then due, at the Rate of Five Pounds per Centum per Annum, without any Deduction, Defalcation, or Abatement whatsoever.

And be it further Enacted by the Authority aforesaid, That from and after the said Twenty-fifth Day of March, One Thousand seven hundred and sixty-two, a separate and distinct Account shall be kept, by the proper Officers, of the Aids and Duties granted by this Act, or any other Act of Parliament now in Force in this Kingdom, and appropriated to particular Uses: And that the Commissioners of His Majesty's Revenue, in their Abstracts, shall return an Account of the several Duties and Taxes so appropriated, and that every Collector, or Receiver of such Duties and Taxes, do take a separate Receipt for the same, when paid into Your Majesty's Treasury, which said Receipt, the Vice-Treasurer or Vice-Treasurers, his or their Deputy or Deputies, is and are hereby required to give accordingly.

CHAP. VI.

AN ACT

FOR

Licensing Hawkers and Pedlars, and for Encouragement of *English* Protestant Schools.

DUBLIN:

Printed by BOULTER GRIERSON, Printer to the King's most Excellent Majesty. MDCCLXII.

AN ACT FOR

Licenſing Hawkers and Pedlars, and for Encouragement of *Engliſh* Proteſtant Schools.

CHAP. VI.

WHEREAS the Continuing the Encouragement formerly given to Engliſh Proteſtant Schools will be of great Benefit to this King‑dom,

CHAP. VI. dom, and it is reasonable that some publick Fund should be applied and set apart for that Purpose; Be it therefore Enacted by the King's Most Excellent Majesty, by and with the Advice and Consent of the Lords Spiritual and Temporal, and Commons in this present Parliament assembled, and by the Authority of the same, that from and after the Twenty-fourth Day of June, One thousand seven hundred and sixty-two, until the Twenty-fourth Day of June, One thousand seven hundred and sixty-four, there shall be answered and paid unto His Majesty, His Heirs and Successors, by every Hawker, Pedlar, petty Chapman, or other trading Person or Persons going from Town to Town, or to other Mens Houses, and travelling either on Foot or with Horse, Horses, or otherwise, within this Kingdom, (except as herein after mentioned) carrying to Sell, or exposing to Sale, any Goods, Wares or Merchandizes, a Duty of Twenty Shillings by the Year, and that every Person so travelling with a Horse, Ass, or Mule, or any other Beast bearing or drawing Burthen, shall pay the Sum of Twenty Shillings by the Year, from the Twenty-fourth Day of June, One thousand seven hundred and sixty-two, to the Twenty-fourth Day of June, One thousand seven hundred and sixty-four, for each

CHAP. VI.

each Horse, Ass, or Mule, or other Beast bearing or drawing Burthen, he or she shall so travel with, over and above the said first mentioned Duty of Twenty Shillings by the Year, which said Rates and Duties shall be collected by such Person and Persons, and in such Manner, and by such Ways and Means, as the Duty payable for Licences to keep Ale-Houses, is raised and collected, by Virtue of an Act made in this Kingdom, in the Thirty-third Year of the Reign of His late Majesty King George the Second, Intituled, An Act for better regulating the Collection of His Majesty's Revenue, and for preventing of Frauds therein, and for repealing an Act made the last Session of Parliament, Intituled, An Act for continuing and amending several Laws heretofore made relating to His Majesty's Revenue, and for the more effectual preventing of Frauds in His Majesty's Customs and Excise, and the several Acts and Statutes which are mentioned in the said Act, and continued thereby, as fully, to all Intents and Purposes, as if the Provisions in the said Act for that Purpose were particularly mentioned and expressed, and enacted again in the Body of this present Act.

And be it further Enacted by the Authority aforesaid, That every Pedlar, Hawker,

Chap.
VI.
per, petty Chapman, and other trading Person or Persons so travelling as aforesaid, shall, before the Twenty-fourth Day of June, One thousand seven hundred and sixty-two, and so likewise in every Year, deliver, or cause to be delivered to the Collector of Excise for the District where he or she shall reside or dwell, a Note in Writing under his or her Hand, or under the Hand of some Person, by her or him authorized in that Behalf, how, and in what Manner he or she intends to travel and trade, whether on Foot, or with one or more Horse or Horses, Ass or Asses, Mule or Mules, or any other Beast bearing or drawing Burthen, for his or her so travelling and trading, for which he or she shall thereupon pay, or cause to be paid unto such Collector, the yearly Duty herein before directed to be payable for the same, and thereupon a Licence shall be granted unto him or her, so to travel or trade, by such Collector.

And be it further Enacted by the Authority aforesaid, That if any such Hawker, Pedlar, or petty Chapman, from and after the said Twenty-fourth Day of June, One thousand seven hundred and sixty-two, be found trading as aforesaid, without, or contrary to such Licence, such Person shall, for each and every such Offence,

fence, forfeit the Sum of Five Pounds, one Moiety thereof to the Informer, and the other Moiety to the Incorporated Society in Dublin for promoting English Protestant Schools.

And be it Enacted by the Authority aforesaid, That it shall and may be lawful, to and for the said Collectors of the several Districts in this Kingdom respectively, and they are hereby respectively directed, appointed and required, upon the Terms aforesaid, and upon the Receipt as aforesaid, to grant a Licence, under their respective Hands, to every Hawker, Pedlar, petty Chapman, or any other trading Person, for him or herself, with one or more Horses, Asses, Mules, or Beasts, which he, she, or they, shall travel with, as the Case shall require, for which Licence there shall be taken by such Collectors, for their own Use, One Shilling, and no more, except such Hawker, Pedlar, or petty Chapman, shall travel with Horse, Ass, or Mule, or any other Beast bearing or drawing Burthen, and in that Case there shall be paid to such Collectors, for their own Use, for such Licence, Two Shillings, and no more, over and above the Duties aforesaid, and that the said Collectors shall keep separate and distinct Accounts of the Duties hereby granted, and

and pay the Money arising thereby into His Majesty's Treasury, as other Money received by them for the Use of His Majesty.

And be it further Enacted by the Authority aforesaid, That the said Collectors shall be accountable to His Majesty for the Duties hereby granted, and shall be subject to the like Penalties and Forfeitures for not rendering a true Account thereof, and paying the same in Manner aforementioned, as they are, and stand liable unto, for not rendering a true Account of any Money received by them for the Use of His Majesty.

And be it further Enacted by the Authority aforesaid, That the Monies arising from the said Duties hereby granted, shall, from Time to Time, be brought into the Receipt of His Majesty's Exchequer, and shall, from Time to Time, without any Fee or Deduction whatsoever, be paid by the Vice-Treasurer, or Receiver-General of this Kingdom, to the Incorporated Society in Dublin for promoting English Protestant Schools, or to their Treasurer for the Time being, for the Use of the said Incorporated Society.

And

And be it further Enacted by the Authority aforesaid, That if any Person or Persons whatsoever shall forge or counterfeit, or cause to be forged or counterfeited, any Licence or Licences for the Purpose aforesaid, or travel with such forged or counterfeited Licence or Licences, knowing the same to be forged and counterfeited, such Person shall forfeit the Sum of Fifty Pounds, One Moiety thereof to the King, and the other Moiety to him who shall prosecute, or sue for the same, to be recovered by Action of Debt, Bill, Plaint, or Information in any of His Majesty's Courts of Record, at the Four-Courts in Dublin, in which no Essoign, Protection, or Wager of Law, or more than one Imparlance shall be allowed, and shall be subject to such other Pains and Penalties, as may be inflicted on Persons for Forgery.

And be it further Enacted by the Authority aforesaid, That if any Person or Persons shall be sued, molested, or troubled for putting in Execution any of the Powers contained in this Act, or for doing any Matter or Thing pursuant thereto, such Person or Persons shall and may plead the General Issue, and give the special Matter in Evidence, and if the Plaintiff

CHAP. VI.

tiff or Plaintiffs shall be nonsuited, or Judgment be given against him or them, upon Demurrer, or otherwise, or a Verdict pass for the Defendant or Defendants, or a Dismiss upon a Civil Bill, such Defendant or Defendants shall have his, her, or their Treble Costs, to be recovered by such Manner, as where by Law Costs are given to Defendants.

And be it further Enacted by the Authority aforesaid, That if any Constable shall refuse or neglect, upon due Notice, or on his own View, to be aiding and assisting in the Execution of this Act, being thereunto required, every such Constable, being thereof convicted by the Oath of One or more credible Witness or Witnesses, before any Justice of the Peace for the County or Place where such Offence shall be committed, shall forfeit for each and every such Offence contrary to this Act, the Sum of Forty Shillings, to be levied by Distress and Sale of the Offenders Goods, by Warrant under the Hand and Seal of such Justice of the Peace, One Moiety whereof to be paid to the said Incorporated Society, the other Moiety to the Informer, Who shall prosecute for the same, rendering the Overplus thereof to the Owner, if any be.

CHAP. VI.

And be it further Enacted by the Authority aforesaid, That it shall and may be lawful for any Person or Persons whatsoever, to seize and detain any such Hawker, Pedlar, Petty Chapman, or other Trading Person or Persons as aforesaid, and also the Goods they shall be found trading with, until such Time as he, she, or they shall produce a Licence in that Behalf, if he, she, or they have any: And if he, she, or they shall be found trading without such Licence, contrary to this Act, that then it shall and may be lawful to and for such Person or Persons so seizing as aforesaid, taking to his or their Assistance, such Person or Persons as he or they shall think fit, to carry the Person so seized, as also the said Goods, before some One of His Majesty's Justices of the Peace of the County or Place, or before the Collector of His Majesty's Revenue, for the District where such Offence or Offences shall be committed, which said Justice of the Peace, and Collector respectively, are hereby strictly required, either upon the Confession of the Party offending, or due Proof of a Witness upon Oath, which they are hereby respectively impowered to administer, that the Person so brought before him, had so traded as aforesaid, unless such Licence shall be produced

by

CHAP. VI.

by such Offender before the said Justice or Collector, by Warrant under his Hand and Seal, to cause the Sum of Five Pounds to be forthwith levied by Distress and Sale of the Offender or Offenders Goods, Wares, or Merchandizes, rendering the Overplus (if any be) to the Owner or Owners thereof, after deducting the reasonable Charge for taking the said Distress, and out of the said Sale to pay the Penalty and Forfeiture aforesaid.

Provided allways, and be it Enacted by the Authority aforesaid, That this Act, or any Thing herein contained, shall not extend to prohibit any Person from selling of any Acts of Parliament, Forms of Prayer, Proclamations, Gazettes, Almanacks, or other printed Papers, or any Fish, Fruit, or Victuals, nor to hinder any Person or Persons, who are the real Workers or Makers of any Goods or Wares within this Kingdom, or his or their Wife or Wives, Apprentice or Apprentices, from carrying abroad, exposing to Sale, and selling any of the said Goods and Wares of his, her, or their making, in any publick Fairs, Markets, or elsewhere, nor any Tinker, Cooper, Glazier, Plumber, Harness-mender, or other Persons, usually trading in mending of Kettles, Tubs, Houshold-Goods,

Goods, or Harness whatsoever, from going about, or carrying with him or them, proper Materials for mending the same.

Provided also, and be it Enacted by the Authority aforesaid, That this Act, or any Thing herein contained, shall not extend to subject any Person or Persons who shall carry raw and unmanufactured Wool or Frizes, or Stockings made of Woolen Yarn, from one Part of the Kingdom to the other, or expose the same to Sale, in any Fair, Market, or other Place in this Kingdom, to any of the Duties or Penalties herein before mentioned, so as such Person or Persons shall not at the same Time, carry, or expose to Sale, any other Goods, Wares, or Merchandizes, except the said raw and unmanufactured Wool, and the said Frizes and Stockings made of Woollen Yarn.

Provided also, and be it Enacted by the Authority aforesaid, That this Act, or any Thing herein contained, shall not extend to prohibit or restrain any Person or Persons from selling or exposing to Sale, in any Place or Places whatsoever, any Flax, Tow, Hemp, Flaxen Yarn, Hempen Yarn, Ticken, plain, striped, chequered, painted, or stained Linens, Buckrams, or Canvas, so as such Person or Persons shall not, at the same Time,

CHAP.
VI.
Time, carry or expose to Sale, any other Goods, Wares, or Merchandizes, except such Flax, Tow, Hemp, Flaxen Yarn, Hempen Yarn, Ticken, plain, striped, chequered, painted, or stained Linens, Buckrams, or Canvass, as aforesaid.

Provided also, and be it Enacted by the Authority aforesaid, That this Act, or any thing herein contained, shall not extend to subject any Person or Persons who shall carry any Pots or Griddles made of Cast Iron Metal, from one Part of the Kingdom to another, or expose the same to Sale in any Fair, Market, or other Place in this Kingdom, to the Payment of any greater Duty than the Sum of Twenty Shillings by the Year in the Whole, although such Person or Persons shall or may trade or travel with one or more Horse or Horses, or other Beast or Beasts, drawing or bearing Burthen, so as such Person or Persons shall not, at the same Time, carry, or expose to Sale, any other Goods, Wares, or Merchandizes, except the said Pots and Griddles, made of Cast Iron Metal.

Provided also, and be it Enacted by the Authority aforesaid, That it shall and may be lawful to and for the Commissioners of his Majesty's Revenue, or any Three or more of them, for the Time being, to order and

and direct to be paid out of the Monies raised by this Act, to the said Collectors, their Clerks, or any other Persons, such Sums of Money, as they, or any of them, shall or may reasonably deserve for their Service, or shall or may have expended in the Execution of, or in relation to this Act.

Provided also, and be it further Enacted by the Authority aforesaid, That this Act, or any thing herein contained, shall not extend, or be construed to give any Power for licensing any Hawker, Pedlar, or Petty Chapman, to sell, or expose to Sale, any Wares or Merchandizes, in any City, Borough, Town-Corporate, or Market-Town within this Realm, any otherwise than he or she might have done before the making of this Act; any thing herein contained to the contrary in any wise notwithstanding.

And for the further Encouragement of English Protestant Schools, Be it Enacted by the Authority aforesaid, That it shall and may be lawful to and for every Arch-Bishop, Bishop, and to and for every Dean Arch-Deacon, Dignitary, Prebendary, Rector, Vicar and Ecclesiastical Person whatsoever, with the Consent of the Arch-Bishop or Bishop of their respective Diocese, signified under the Hand and Seal of such Arch-Bishop and Bishop respectively, and to

CHAP. VI.

and for every Person being seized of an Estate for Life, in Possession of any Land, with immediate Remainder over to his Issue in Tail, by Deed or Deeds respectively, to grant in Possession absolutely, or in Fee Farm, any Quantity of Land to them respectively belonging, not exceeding two Acres, Plantation Measure, to the said Incorporated Society, and their Successors for ever, and that all Grants so to be made, shall be good and effectual against the Successors of such Arch-Bishop, Bishop, Dean, Arch-Deacon, Dignitary, Prebendary, Rector, Vicar, and other Ecclesiastical Person respectively, and against all Persons claiming, or to claim any Estate, Right, Title or Interest in such Land, by Virtue of, or under any Limitation, Remainder, or Reversion, expectant upon such Estate for Life.

CHAP. VII.

AN ACT

FOR

Continuing and Amending an Act, Intituled, *An Act for better Regulating the Collection of His Majesty's Revenue, and for Preventing Frauds therein*; and for repealing an Act made the last Session of Parliament, Intituled, *An Act for Continuing and Amending several Laws heretofore made, relating to His Majesty's Revenue, and for the more effectual Preventing of Frauds in His Majesty's Customs and Excise*, and the several Acts and Statutes which are mentioned in the said Act, and continued thereby.

DUBLIN:
Printed by BOULTER GRIERSON, Printer to the King's Most Excellent Majesty. MDCCLXII.

(103)

AN ACT

FOR

Continuing and Amending an Act, Intituled, *An Act for better Regulating the Collection of His Majesty's Revenue, and for preventing Frauds therein;* and for Repealing an Act made the last Session of Parliament, Intituled, *An Act for Continuing and Amending several Laws heretofore made, relating to His Majesty's Revenue, and for the more effectual preventing of Frauds in His Majesty's Customs and Excise,* and the several Acts and Statutes which are mentioned in the said Act, and continued thereby.

CHAP. VII.

WHEREAS by an Act passed in the Thirty-third Year of the Reign of His late Majesty King George the Second, Intituled, An Act for the better regulating

CHAP. VII. regulating the Collection of His Majesty's Revenue, and for preventing of Frauds therein; and for Repealing an Act made the last Session of Parliament, Intituled, An Act for Continuing and Amending several Laws heretofore made, relating to His Majesty's Revenue, and for the more effectual preventing of Frauds in His Majesty's Customs and Excise, and the several Acts and Statutes which are mentioned in the said Act, and continued thereby; several Provisions were made for regulating the Collection of His Majesty's Revenue, and preventing Frauds therein, which have been found to be of general Use, but are now near expiring; Be it Enacted by the King's Most Excellent Majesty, by and with the Advice and Consent of the Lords Spiritual and Temporal, and Commons in this present Parliament Assembled, and by the Authority of the same, That the said recited Act, and all and every the Clause and Clauses therein contained (except such Parts thereof as are altered or repealed by this present Act) shall continue and be in Force for the Space of Two Years, from the Twenty-fourth Day of June, One thousand seven hundred and sixty-two, and from thence to the End of the then next Session of Parliament, and no longer.

And whereas by the said recited Act, passed in the Thirty third Year of the Reign of of His late Majesty King George the Second, It is among other Things Enacted, That from and after the Twenty-fourth Day of June, One thousand seven hundred and sixty, it should and might be lawful to and for the Chief Commissioners of His Majesty's Excise, or any Three of them, and the Collectors of His Majesty's Excise, in their several Districts, from Time to Time, to take Recognizances, and to issue and grant Licences for selling of Beer, Ale, Wine, Strong Waters, and Spirits respectively, in such Manner as in and by the said Act is directed.

And Whereas a Doubt hath arisen, whether the Chief Commissioners of His Majesty's Excise, or any Three of them, are impowered by the said recited Act, to issue and grant such Licences in any other District than in the District of the Excise-Office of the City, and County of the City of Dublin, and County of Dublin; For Remedy whereof, and for obviating and taking away all Doubts relative to the granting of such Licences, Be it Enacted and Declared by the Authority aforesaid, That it shall and may be lawful to and for the Chief Commissioners of Excise, for the Time being, or any Three or more of them, to issue and grant Licences for selling of Beer, Ale, Wine, Strong Waters, and Spirits respectively,

CHAP. VII.

spectively, in all, or any of the Counties and Districts of this Kingdom, to such Person or Persons as they, or any Three or more of them, in their Discretion shall think fit.

Provided nevertheless, That before any Licence shall be delivered to the Person or Persons applying for the same, such and the like Recognizances as are mentioned and appointed to be taken by the said recited Act, shall be acknowledged before the Collector of Excise, in the District where the Person or Persons applying for such Licences, doth or shall reside, who is hereby authorized and impowered to take the same; and the Collectors of Excise, in their several and respective Districts, are hereby required to make a Return of such Recognizances to the Clerks of the Peace, or their Deputies, in such and the same Manner, as in and by the said recited Act is directed and appointed, with Regard to the Recognizances therein mentioned.

And whereas by the said recited Act, It is Enacted, That from and after the Twenty-fourth Day of June, One thousand seven hundred and sixty, all Aqua Vitæ, Spirits, or Strong Waters, exceeding in Quantity more than four Gallons, that shall be carried or conveyed from any Place

in

in this Kingdom, to any Part thereof by Inland Carriage, should be liable to be seized by any of the Officers of His Majesty's Revenue, and should be deemed and taken to be unlawfully distilled, and forfeited as such, unless the Person carrying such Aqua Vitæ, Spirits, or Strong Waters, should produce a Permit or Let-pass, given and signed by some one of the Officers of Excise, within the District from whence such Aqua Vitæ, Spirits, or Strong Waters were intended to be carried.

And whereas it has been found, That the Provisions made in and by the said recited Acts, relative to Permits, or Let-passes, for conveying such Spirits, have proved ineffectual; Be it therefore Enacted by the Authority aforesaid, That from and after the Twenty-fourth Day of June, One thousand seven hundred and sixty two, it shall and may be lawful to and for any Officer of His Majesty's Revenue, to enter in the Day time into all or any of the Houses, Out-houses, Store-houses, or other Places Whatsoever, of or belonging to any Person or Persons who shall sell any Aqua Vitæ, Spirits, or Strong Waters, or Simple or Compound Waters, made or distilled in this Kingdom, either by Wholesale or Retail (other than and except Apothecaries and Druggists) and there to demand a Permit

CHAP. VII.

or Let-pass (signed by some one of the Officers of Excise in the District where such Aqua Vitæ, Spirits, or Strong Waters shall be made or distilled) for each and every Cask, or other Vessel containing more than Four Gallons of Aqua Vitæ, Spirits, or Strong Waters, made or distilled in this Kingdom, that shall be found or discovered in the Custody or Possession of such Person or Persons. And if on Demand made by such Officer as aforesaid, no Permit or Let-pass, signed as aforesaid, shall be produced within a reasonable Time after such Demand made, or Proof made that a Permit had been granted for the same, and was afterwards lost or mislaid, then all the Aqua Vitæ, Spirits, or Strong Waters in such Casks, or other Vessels, containing more than Four Gallons, shall be seized, and shall be deemed and taken to be unlawfully distilled, and forfeited as such, together with the Cask or Vessel in which such Aqua Vitæ, Spirits, or Strong Waters shall be contained.

And be it further Enacted by the Authority aforesaid, That from and after the first Day of May, One thousand seven hundred and sixty two, it shall and may be lawful to and for the Gaugers, and other Officers of Excise, to visit, in the Day Time, the Sugar-Houses of or belonging to any

Sugar-

Sugar-baker, and there to take an Account of all Sugar-water Wash which shall be found in the Houses, Out-houses, or Yards of such Sugar-baker, and upon any Decrease afterwards found therein, to charge such Sugar-baker with the Duty charged upon Wash of Molosses, or of Sugar, unless such Sugar-baker shall declare the Name or Names, and the Place or Places of Abode, of the Person or Persons to whom he sold or delivered the same.

And for preventing Frauds that are daily practised by Persons hiring out private Brew-houses, and Utensils for Brewing, in order to evade the Payment of the Duties of Excise; Be it further Enacted by the Authority aforesaid, That from and after the Twenty-fourth Day of June, One thousand seven hundred and sixty-two, no Person or Persons shall let out to Hire, or lend any private Brew-house, either with or without Utensils for Brewing, to any Person or Persons whatsoever, unless the Person or Persons so letting out for Hire, or lending such Private Brew-house, shall obtain an annual Licence for so doing, from the Commissioners of His Majesty's Excise, or any Three or more of them, or from the Collector of the District wherein such private Brew-house shall be situated, for which Licence, before the same shall be granted,

CHAP. VII. granted, there shall be paid to and for the Use of His Majesty, His Heirs and Successors, the Sum of Fifty Pounds Sterling; and in Case any Person or Persons shall let out to Hire, or lend any private Brew-house, either with or without Utensils for Brewing, without such Licence first had and obtained, then, and in every such Case so happening, the Person or Persons so letting out to Hire, or lending a private Brew-house, and the Person or Persons to whom the same shall be so let to Hire, or lent, shall respectively forfeit the Sum of Fifty Pounds Sterling, to be recovered in Manner herein after mentioned.

And be it further Enacted by the Authority aforesaid, That from and after the Twenty-fourth Day of June, One thousand seven hundred and sixty two, all Stills, Black Pots, and Alembicks, containing more than Twelve Gallons, shall, before the same are set at Work, be entered and registered in the Office of Excise, of the District wherein such Still, Black Pot, or Alembick is intended to be wrought, which Entry or Registry shall contain the Christian Name and Surname of the Distiller, the true Contents of the Still, Black Pot, or Alembick, and the Place where such Still, Black Pot, or Alembick is fixed, or intended to be fixed, and the Day of the Month when such Registry is made, for which

which Entry a Fee of Six Pence shall be paid, and no more, and the Officer of Excise shall thereupon grant a Certificate thereof: And if any Still, Black Pot, or Alembick, which shall hold or contain more than Twelve Gallons, shall, after the said Twenty fourth Day of June, One thousand seven hundred and sixty two, be found or discovered in the House or Possession of any Person or Persons (other than and except a Brazier, or other Manufacturer in Metal) not entered or registered in Manner aforesaid; then every such Still, Black Pot, or Alembick, shall be seized and forfeited, and all Wash and Pot-Ale, which shall be found therein, shall be spilled, and all Low Wines and Strong Waters found therein, shall be likewise forfeited.

And be it further Enacted by the Authority aforesaid, That from and after the said Twenty fourth Day of June, One thousand seven hundred and sixty two, no Person or Persons shall have or keep in his, her, or their Custody or Possession, or shall make Use of any Backs or other Vessels for fermenting Wash of Molosses or Sugar, which shall not hold or contain Four Hundred Gallons at the least, upon Pain of forfeiting such Backs, or other Vessels, and also the Sum of Ten Pounds for every such

CHAP. VII. Offence, to be recovered in Manner herein after mentioned.

And Whereas it frequently happens, that Houses and Ground fit and convenient for building Custom-Houses, and other Houses for the Service of the Revenue, are wanted, but by reason of some Disability in the Person or Persons seized or interested in the same, no absolute Sale, or Demise for a long Term of Years, can be obtained therein, which has often proved very inconvenient and prejudicial to His Majesty's Service; Be it further Enacted by the Authority aforesaid, That from and after the said Twenty fourth Day of June, One thousand seven hundred and sixty two, it shall and may be lawful for all Persons, Bodies Politick and Corporate, Tenants in Tail, Tenants for Life, With Remainders to their Sons, or Issue in Tail, Infants, by their Guardians, the Guardians and Committees of Lunaticks and Idcots, Femes Covert, with their Husbands, by Deeds indented and inrolled, to demise for any Term of Years to His Majesty, or to such Person or Persons as the Chief Commissioners of His Majesty's Revenue, for the Time being, or any Three or more of them, shall appoint, any Ground, Lands, or Tenements, necessary or convenient for building Custom-houses, or other Houses and Yards for the Service of the Revenue

(not

(not exceeding One Acre Plantation Measure) and not being Part of the Demesnes usually occupied with the Mansion-house of the Person or Persons so demising the same.

And be it further Enacted by the Authority aforesaid, That every such Demise that shall be made as aforesaid, of any Grounds, Lands, or Tenements, necessary or convenient for building Custom-houses, or other Houses for the Service of the Revenue, with all Ways, Yards, Passages, and Appurtenances, shall be valid and effectual in Law, notwithstanding any Disability or Incapacity whatsoever, in the Person or Persons demising the same.

Provided nevertheless, That no Lease, Contract, or Demise, hereafter to be made, by Tenants for Life, or Infants by their Guardians, or by the Guardians and Committees of Lunaticks and Ideots, shall be deemed valid and effectual in the Law, unless the Lord Chancellor, or Lord Keeper of the Great Seal in Ireland, for the Time being, do, by Writing indorsed on such Lease, Contract, or Demise, signify his Consent and Approbation of the same.

CHAP. VII. And to the Intent that the several and respective Owners and Proprietors of all such Ground, Lands, or Tenements, their several and respective Heirs, Executors, Administrators and Assigns, may be well and truly paid the yearly Rents that shall be agreed upon for the same; Be it Enacted by the Authority aforesaid, That the said yearly Rents shall be inserted on the Revenue List of Incident Expences, according to such Contracts and Agreements, and be paid, and payable unto such Owners and Proprietors, their several and respective Heirs, Executors, Administrators and Assigns, according to their several and respective Estates and Interests in the Ground, Lands, or Tenements, to be demised without any Deduction, Defalcation, or Abatement Whatsoever; and that the Commissioners of the Revenue, for the Time being, or any Three or more of them, shall pay, or cause to be paid out of His Majesty's Revenue, under their Direction and Management, the said yearly Rents, according to such Contracts or Demises, from Time to Time yearly, or half yearly, as the said Rent shall be contracted for, unto such Owners and Proprietors, their several and respective Heirs, Executors, Administrators and Assigns, in Manner and Form aforesaid, according to the true Intent and Meaning of this Act.

Provided

CHAP. VII.

Provided always, and be it further Enacted by the Authority aforesaid, That nothing herein contained, shall in any way impeach or prejudice, or be construed, deemed, or taken to impeach or prejudice, any former Agreements, Contracts, or Demises, heretofore at any Time made, for, or concerning any Lands, Tenements, or Hereditaments, whereon any Custom-houses, or other Houses for the Service of the Revenue, have been built, or are now building, or hereafter shall be built; but, that during the Continuance of such Agreements, Contracts, or Demises, the same shall continue, be, and remain in the same Force and Validity, as if this Act had not been made; any Thing herein contained to the Contrary notwithstanding.

And whereas great Inconveniencies have arisen, for want of fit Persons being authorized to take and receive Affidavits in the several Counties of this Kingdom, in Causes or Proceedings before the Commissioners of Appeal; Be it Enacted by the Authority aforesaid, That it shall and may be lawful, to and for the Commissioners of Appeal, or any Two of them, by Commission under their Hands and Seals, from Time to Time, to authorize and impower such Person or Persons

CHAP. VII. sons as they shall think fit, in the several Counties of this Kingdom, to be Commissioners to take and receive Affidavits, concerning any Cause depending, or other Proceedings in Causes of Appeal, before the Commissioners of Appeal; and all Affidavits taken as aforesaid, shall be of the same Force as Affidavits taken before the said Commissioners of Appeal are, or may be, and for the swearing and taking of every such Affidavit, the Persons so impowered, or taking the same, shall receive a Fee of One Shilling and Six-pence, and no more.

And be it further Enacted by the Authority aforesaid, That every Person who shall make such Affidavit as aforesaid, and shall be lawfully convicted of having wilfully, falsely, and corruptly sworn any Matter or Thing in such Affidavit contained, shall incur and be subject to the same Penalties and Forfeitures, as by the Laws and Statutes of this Kingdom are Enacted against Persons convicted of wilful and corrupt Perjury.

And be it further Enacted by the Authority aforesaid, That no Affidavit taken by any Commissioner authorized as aforesaid, shall be read or made use of before the Commissioners of Appeal, unless the Commissioner,

Commissioner, or Person that takes the same, mention in the Caption thereof, the Day of the Month when, and also the Place and County where, the same shall be sworn, and that he knows the Deponent, or has been credibly informed that he is the real Person mentioned and described in such Affidavit.

CHAP. VII.

And Whereas by an Act passed in this Kingdom, in the Fourteenth and Fifteenth Years of the Reign of King Charles the Second, Intituled, An Act for settling of the Excise or New Impost upon His Majesty, His Heirs and Successors, according to the Book of Rates therein inserted, it was (among other Things) Enacted and Ordained, That there should be an Office constituted and erected in the City of Dublin, to be called and known by the Name of the Office of Excise, or New Impost, to be managed and governed by Commissioners, not exceeding Five in Number, and also a Surveyor, all to be appointed by the Lord Lieutenant, Lord Deputy, or other Chief Governor or Governors of Ireland for the Time being, and to be commissioned under the Great Seal of this Realm, to have and to hold to them respectively, during their good Behaviour respectively.

G g And

CHAP. VII. **And Whereas by One other Act of Parliament made in this Kingdom, in the said Fourteenth and Fifteenth Years of the Reign of the said King** Charles the Second, **Intituled,** An Act for settling the Subsidy of Poundage, and granting a Subsidy of Tunnage, and other Sums of Money unto His Royal Majesty, His Heirs and Successors, the same to be paid upon Merchandizes imported and exported, according to a Book of Rates hereunto annexed, **it was (among other Things) Enacted, That the Book of Rates, together with certain Rules, Orders, and Directions thereunto annexed, Intituled,** Certain Rules, Orders, Directions, and Allowances for the Advancement of Trade, and the Encouragement of Merchants, and also for the regulating, as well of the Merchants in making of due Entries and just Payments of their Customs, as of the Officers in all Ports of this Realm, in the Receipts of their several Fees, and in the faithful Management of their Duties and Trusts; **and every Article, Clause, Sentence, and Rule, in the before-mentioned Book of Rates, and certain Rules, Orders, and Directions aforesaid, should, from and after the First Day of** December, **One thousand six hundred and sixty-one, be and remain as effectual, to all Intents and Purposes, as** as if the same had been particularly included in the Body of the said Act.

And whereas by the forty-seventh Rule annexed to the said Book of Rates, it was ordered, That for the better Management, as well as lessening the Charge of His Majesty's Revenue, the Commissioners of the Customs should not at any Time, be more than Seven, or less than Five in Number, to be appointed from Time to Time by the Lord Lieutenant, Lord Deputy, or other Chief Governor or Governors, and Privy Council of this Realm, and known unto them for Persons of Ability and Experience in Custom Affairs, who should have Commission under the great Seal of this Kingdom, during Pleasure only.

And whereas for many Years past the Commissioners of Excise, as well as the Commissioners of the Customs, have been appointed by one Commission under the Great Seal of this Kingdom, to hold their respective Offices during His Majesty's Pleasure only, pursuant to Letters for that Purpose, under the Sign Manual of His Majesty and His Predecessors.

And whereas it has been of late questioned, Whether the Appointment of the Commissioners

CHAP. VII. Commissioners of Excise by His Majesty, and during His Majesty's pleasure only, be strictly legal, Be it Enacted by the Authority aforesaid, That all and every the Commissions and Letters Patent, which have heretofore been passed under the Great Seal of this Kingdom, constituting and appointing the several and respective Persons named or mentioned in such Commissions or Letters Patent respectively, Commissioners of Excise, or Commissioners of Customs, shall be, and are hereby declared to be firm, valid, and effectual in the Law, to all Intents and Purposes whatsoever.

And be it further Enacted by the Authority aforesaid, That from Time to Time, and at all Times for ever hereafter, it shall and may be lawful for His Majesty, His Heirs and Successors, to constitute and appoint Commissioners of the Excise, and Commissioners of the Customs, by One or more Commission or Commissions, under the Great Seal of this Kingdom, to have and to hold their respective Offices or Places during their good Behaviour respectively, or during His Majesty's Pleasure only, as to his Majesty, His Heirs and Successors, shall seem fitting; which Commissioners so appointed, or to be appointed, shall respectively have all such Powers

Powers and Authorities, as the Commissioners of Excise, and Commissioners of Customs, respectively, are now intituled to have, use, or exercise, by any Law now in Force in this Kingdom.

And Whereas by the Act of Excise, or New Impost, it is enacted, That all Goods and Merchandizes seized for being run, or intended to be run, shall be brought to the Office of Excise next adjoining to the Place where such Goods shall be so seized, there to be detained and kept, until the same shall be condemned or discharged, in Manner as by the said Act of Excise is provided, Which has, in many Cases, been attended with Inconveniencies, and Damage to the Owners of such Goods and Merchandizes, by losing their Market, before a Trial could be had thereon; and many Disadvantages have also arisen, by the Detention of Ships or Vessels laden with such Goods and Commodities, and thereby preventing them from proceeding on their intended Voyages; For Remedy whereof, Be it Enacted by the Authority aforesaid, That from and after the First Day of May, One thousand seven hundred and sixty-two, it shall and may be lawful, to and for the Owner or Owners of any Goods and Merchandizes, seized for being run, or intended to be

CHAP. VII.

be tun, and to and for the Master or Commander of any Ship or Vessel seized for the Breach of any of the Laws of Excise, to apply (as by Law may now be done, in Cases to be heard and determined in the Court of Exchequer) for a Writ of Appraisement, to value and appraise such Goods and Merchandizes, and Ship or Vessel so seized, on which such Proceedings shall and may be had, as have been usual in Cases where by Law Writs of Appraisement have issued, and on Return of the Appraisement, or Value of such Goods and Commodities, and of such Ships and Vessels, the Party or Parties applying for such Writ of Appraisement, together with Two sufficient Sureties, shall enter into a Recognizance to His Majesty in double the Value of such Appraisement, before the Chancellor, or One of the Barons of the Court of Exchequer, or before such other Person or Persons as they, or any of them, shall appoint, by Commission to be issued out of the said Court of Exchequer, conditioned to pay such appraised Value, and all other Penalties and Forfeitures attending such Seizure, in Case the same shall be condemned; and thereupon the said Chancellor, or any of the said Barons of the said Court of Exchequer, shall award a Writ of Delivery in the usual Manner, for such Goods and

Merchandizes,

Merchandizes, and the Ship or Vessel so seized as aforesaid.

Provided allways, That upon the Acquittal of such Goods and Merchandizes, and Ships or Vessels from such Seizure as aforesaid, by the Chief Commissioners of the Revenue, or their Sub-Commissioners, in their several and respective Districts, or by the Commissioners of Appeal (in Case an Appeal shall be brought) and due Proof made thereof before the said Chancellor, or any of the Barons of the said Court of Exchequer, and Notice given to his Majesty's Attorney General for the Time being, that then the said Chancellor, or any of the Barons of the said Court of Exchequer, shall and may, and they are hereby required and directed to order the said Recognizance to be vacated, and the same shall afterwards be null and void to all Intents and Purposes whatsoever.

And be it further Enacted by the Authority aforesaid, That all the Forfeitures and Penalties inflicted by this Act, shall and may be sued for, and recovered, levied, and applied in such Manner and Form, and by such Ways and Methods, as are prescribed and appointed in and by the said Act, made in the Fourteenth and Fifteenth Years

CHAP. VII. Years of the Reign of King Charles the Second, Intituled, An Act for settling of the Excise or New Impost upon His Majesty, His Heirs and Successors, according to the Book of Rates therein inserted; With the like Remedy of Appeal to the Party or Parties that shall think him or themselves aggrieved or injured, as by the said Act is provided.

Provided always, and be it Enacted by the Authority aforesaid, That so much of this Act as is made for continuing and amending any former Act of Parliament for the Improvement of His Majesty's Revenue, and the several further Provisions hereby made for the like Purposes, shall continue and be in Force for Two Years, from the Twenty-fourth Day of June, One thousand seven hundred and sixty-two, and from thence to the End of the then next Session of Parliament, and no longer: But that the several Clauses in this present Act contained, relative to the Appointment of the Commissioners of Excise and Customs, shall be, and is hereby declared to be perpetual.

CHAP. VIII.

AN
ACT
TO
Enable Tenants for Life to make perpetual Leases of Grounds whereon to erect Publick Hospitals.

DUBLIN:

Printed by BOULTER GRIERSON, Printer to the King's most Excellent Majesty. MDCCLXII.

AN ACT TO

Enable Tenants for Life to make perpetual Leafes of Grounds whereon to erect Publick Hofpitals.

CHAP. VIII.

Be it Enacted by the King's Most Excellent Majesty, by and with the Advice and Consent of the Lords Spiritual and Temporal, and Commons in this present Parliament assembled, and by the Authority of the same, That it shall and may be lawful, to and for any Tenant for Life of Lands near any City or Town Corporate, fit for the Purpose of building an Hospital for sick or maimed Persons,

CHAP. VIII.

Persons, by Deed indented, to demise to any Person or Persons for erecting such Hospital, any such Lands not exceeding in the Whole, by the Demise of any one such Lessor, an Acre of Ground Plantation Measure, for any Term of Years, or with Covenants for perpetual Renewal, reserving a Rent according to the full improved Value, payable to those Who are or shall be intitled to the Freehold and Inheritance, and such Lease and Leases shall be good and valid against all Persons in Remainder, after such Tenants for Life, or claiming under such Remainder-men.

Provided that it shall and may be in the Power of the Person or Persons intitled to the first Estate of Inheritance in Remainder, after the Determination of the Estate of such Tenant for Life, to appoint and allot such particular Acre, Part of such Lands as he, she, or they, shall think most convenient to be demised.

Provided also, that such Hospital be erected on such Lands within the Space of Three Years next after the Execution of such Lease, otherwise such Lease shall not be binding upon any of the Persons in Remainder, after such Tenant for Life.

A N

AN ACT

TO

Prevent the Counterfeiting Gold and Silver Lace, and for Settling and Adjusting the Proportions of fine Gold, Silver, and Silk, and for the better making of Gold and Silver Thread.

CHAP. IX.

WHEREAS hitherto there has not been any Law in this Kingdom for ascertaining the Fineness of Silver, and Quantity of Gold to be laid thereon in making Wire for

CHAP.
IX.
Threads, and the other Denominations necessary in manufacturing Gold and Silver Lace, nor for proportioning the Quantity and Quality of Silk, to be used in the same, by which Frauds may be committed, to the great Loss of His Majesty's Subjects, and Hurt and Damage to the Trade of this Kingdom: For Remedy whereof, Be it Enacted by the King's most Excellent Majesty, by and with the Advice and Consent of the Lords Spiritual and Temporal, and Commons in this present Parliament assembled, and by the Authority of the same, That from and after the First Day of May, One thousand seven hundred and sixty two, all Copper, Brass, and every other Metal inferior to Silver, shall be spun upon Thread Yarn or Incle only, and not spun, mixed, wove, wrought, or set upon Silk, upon Pain, that each and every Person offending therein, shall forfeit and pay the Sum of Five Shillings for each and every Ounce so spun, mixed, wove, wrought, or set upon Silk.

Be it further Enacted by the Authority aforesaid, That from and after the said First Day of May, all Silver Wire to be drawn for the making of Silver Thread, shall hold at least Eleven Ounces Fifteen Penny

Penny Weight of fine Silver upon the Pound Weight Troy, and that all Silver to be gilt, and made Use of in the Wire-Drawers Trade, shall hold at least Eleven Ounces Ten Penny Weight of fine Silver upon the Pound Weight Troy, and shall not have less than Four Penny Weight Four Grains of fine Gold, without any Allay, laid upon each Pound Weight of the said Silver, upon Pain, that the Refiner, or Maker thereof, shall forfeit and pay the Sum of Five Shillings for each and every Ounce so made, contrary to the Directions of this Act.

Be it further Enacted by the Authority aforesaid, That from and after the said First Day of May, no gilt Wire shall be coloured with Verdegrease, or Dead-Head, or any other Force Colour, upon Pain, that the Person so offending, shall forfeit and pay the Sum of Two Shillings and Six Pence, for every Ounce so coloured, and for all Gold and Silver prepared as aforesaid, and reduced into Plate, there shall be allowed, at the least, Six Ounces of the said Plate, to cover Four Ounces of Silk, except large Twist, Freeze, Freezon, Frost, and Cheque, and also except round Brocade, used in the making Brocaded Gold and Silver Silks or Stuffs only, in which there shall be allowed, at the least, Six Ounces of the said Plate, to cover Five Ounces of Silk, and no more; all which Gold and Silver Plate shall be spun close upon well boiled and light dyed Silk only, except Frost, being run thin, and spun upon different coloured Silk; And in case any Spinner of Gold and Silver Thread, or other Person, shall lay Gold or Silver Plate upon any greater Proportions of Silk, or in any other Manner, than as before directed by this Act (Except as is herein before is excepted) such Spinner, or other Person, shall forfeit and pay Two Shillings and Six Pence for every Ounce so spun.

Be it further Enacted by the Authority aforesaid, That if any Person whatsoever, from and after the said First Day of May, shall sell, or offer to Sale, any Gold or Silver Orrice Lace, mixed with any other Metal or Materials than Gold or Silver, Silk and Uellum, the Person so selling, or offering the same to Sale, shall forfeit and pay, for every Ounce, the Sum of Two Shilling and Six Pence.

Be it further Enacted by the Authority aforesaid, That if any Person whatsoever, after the said First Day of May, shall sell any Gold or Silver Wire, Plate, Thread, Lace,

Lace, or Fringe, by any other Weight than Troy Weight, the Person so selling, shall forfeit, for every Ounce so sold, the Sum of Five Shillings.

Be it further Enacted by the Authority aforesaid, That from and after the said First Day of May, if any Maker, or Seller of any Goods, made or mixed with Gold or Silver Thread, or Plate, shall make or sell any Goods mixed with Gold or Silver Thread, or Plate, made contrary to the Intent and Meaning of this Act, such Person or Persons shall forfeit and pay Five Shillings for each and every Ounce of Gold and Silver Thread, or Plate, so made or Sold.

Be it further Enacted by the Authority aforesaid, That from and after the said First Day of May, no Gold or Silver Thread, Lace, Fringe, or any other Work made thereof, or any Thread, Lace, Fringe, or other Work made of Copper, Brass, or any other inferior Metal, or Gold or Silver Wire, or Plate, not of the Manufacture of Great Britain, shall be imported, upon Pain of being forfeited and burned, and upon the further Penalty of One Hundred Pounds, to be paid by the Importer thereof, for each and every Parcel so imported.

CHAP. IX.

Be it further Enacted by the Authority aforesaid, That of the several Penalties and Forfeitures made and inflicted by this Act, One Moiety shall be to the Use of His Majesty, His Heirs and Successors, and the other Moiety to him, her, or them, that shall inform, sue, or prosecute for the same, and may be sued for, and recovered, by Action of Debt, Bill, Plaint, or Information, in any of His Majesty's Courts of Record in Dublin, wherein no Essoign, Protection, Privilege, or Wager of Law, or more than one Imparlance shall be allowed.

Be it further Enacted by the Authority aforesaid, That if any Person or Persons shall be sued for what either he, she, or they shall do, in the Execution of this Act, he, she, or they, may plead the General Issue, and give this Act, and the Special Matter in Evidence, and if the Plaintiff or Plaintiffs shall become nonsuit, or discontinue his, her, or their Action or Actions, or if a Verdict shall pass against him, her, or them, the Defendant or Defendants shall recover treble Costs, for which they shall have the like Remedy, as in other Cases where Costs are allowed to Defendants.

Provided

Provided always, That every Suit, Action, or Prosecution, to be brought by Virtue of this Act, shall be commenced within Six Kalendar Months after the Offence committed.

Provided always, That nothing in this Act contained, shall be construed to Inflict any Penalty upon any Person for selling, or exposing to Sale, any Silver Wire, or Silver or Gold Thread, or any Lace, or Fringe, on or before the First Day of May, One thousand seven hundred and sixty three, though the same be not made according to the Rules and Directions of this Act.

Provided proof be made, by Oath of one or more credible Witness or Witnesses, before some Justice of the Peace of the County, City, Town or Place where the same shall be sold, or exposed to sale (which Oath the said Justice is hereby impowered and required to administer) that such Goods are really, and bona fide, the Manufacture of this Kingdom, and were made on or before the said First Day of May, One thousand seven hundred and sixty three.

Provided also, That nothing in this Act contained, shall extend, or be construed to

CHAP. IX.

Chap. IX. extend, to prohibit any Copper, Brass, or any other metal, inferior to Silver, spun upon Thread, Yarn or Inkle, as this Act directs, being wrought or sewed with Silk, upon any Garment or Apparel actually used in Theatrical Entertainments only.

Be it Enacted by the Authority aforesaid, That this Act shall be deemed, adjudged, and taken to be, a publick Act, and shall be judicially taken Notice of as such, by all Judges, Justices, and other Persons whatsoever, without specially pleading the same.

CHAP. X.

AN

ACT

TO

Prevent the exceffive Price of Coals in the City of *Dublin*.

DUBLIN:

Printed by BOULTER GRIERSON, Printer to the King's Moft Excellent Majefty. MDCCLXII.

AN ACT

TO

Prevent the excessive Price of Coals in the City of *Dublin*.

CHAP. X.

WHEREAS several persons in the said City make a Practice of buying up intire Cargoes of Coals before they are brought up to the Quay,

CHAP. X. Quay, or publick Landing Place, and by these Means engross large Quantities of Coals, and afterwards retail the same at exorbitant Prices.

And whereas by the several Frauds practised in the Coal Trade, the Poor of this City have been reduced to great Distress: For Remedy whereof, be it Enacted by the King's Most Excellent Majesty, by and with the Advice and Consent of the Lords Spiritual and Temporal, and Commons in this present Parliament assembled, and by the Authority of the same, That from and after the first Day of May, in the Year One thousand seven hundred and sixty-two, no Person shall be allowed to purchase Coals for Sale, or to keep any Yard for selling Coals, or to act as a Factor, Purser, or Agent for buying or selling Coals in the said City, without having a Licence for that Purpose, signed by the Lord Mayor or Recorder of the said City; and no Licence shall be granted, unless the Person desiring such Licence, shall first enter into Bond, with sufficient Security, of the Penalty of Two Hundred Pounds, conditioned for such Persons not being in any Sort concerned in Engrossing, Forestalling, or Regrating, or in any Combination for raising the Price of Coals, for which Licence, and also

also for filling up the said Bond, One Shilling, and no more, shall be paid.

CHAP. X.

And be it Enacted by the Authority aforesaid, That the said Factors, Pursers, or Agents, shall never exceed the Number of Forty, and shall never buy any Coals to sell again; and that no such Factor, Purser, or Agent, shall buy in any One Year for his own Consumption, a greater Quantity than Twenty Tuns; and every Person who shall keep any Yard for selling Coals, without first obtaining such Licence, and every Factor, or Purser, or Agent, who shall buy any Coals to sell again, shall, for every such Offence, forfeit One Hundred Pounds.

And be it Enacted by the Authority aforesaid, That every such Factor, Agent, or Purser, shall take an Oath, to be administered by the Lord Mayor of the City of Dublin (which Oath the said Lord Mayor is hereby impowered to administer) that he will not, during the Time of his being Factor, Pursur, or Agent, buy any Coals to sell again, and that he will exercise the said Office faithfully, diligently, and impartially, between the Seller and Buyers of Coals.

CHAP. X.

And be it Enacted by the Authority aforesaid, That no Person who shall keep a Coal Yard, or be concerned as a Factor, Purser, or Agent, shall keep any Lighter, Gabbard, or Boat, for the Purpose of carrying Coals; and that no Person shall keep such Boat or Gabbard, without having a Written Licence for that Purpose, signed by the Lord Mayor or Recorder of this City, for which Licence, One Shilling, and no more, shall be paid; and every Person who shall offend herein, shall, for every such Offence, forfeit the Sum of One Hundred Pounds.

And be it Enacted by the Authority aforesaid, That the Master of every Vessel shall be obliged, immediately on the Arrival of every such Vessel at any of the Quays, or Publick Landing Places of this City, to hang at the Mast of his said Vessel, or of the Lighter, Gabbard, or Boat, in which Coals shall be brought up to the said Quays or Landing-Places, a Board, with the true Name of the Place from whence the said Coals were brought, written thereupon in large legible Characters; and no Sum of Money shall be charged or taken, by any Person whatsoever, for hanging out such Board; and every Person who shall keep a Yard for selling

ling Coals in the City of Dublin, shall hang at the Door of said Yard a Board, the Denomination of the Coals then contained in said Yard, written in large legible Characters; and every Person offending herein, shall forfeit the Sum of Twenty Pounds. And every Master, Factor, or Porter, and every Person keeping a Yard for selling Coals, and every Person whatsoever, who shall knowingly or wilfully sell Coals by a false Denomination, or impose, or be any ways aiding or instrumental in imposing upon any Buyer of Coals, touching the Denomination or Kind of the said Coals, shall, for every such Offence, forfeit the Sum of Fifty Pounds.

And for preventing the Frauds practised by Measurers, Porters, and Carmen, Be it Enacted by the Authority aforesaid, That the Lord Mayor, Recorder, and Board of Aldermen of the said City, or the Majority of them, shall have Power, from Time to Time, to make such Rules and By-Laws for fixing the Wages, and regulating the Conduct of Measurers, Porters, and Carmen, employed in the Carriage or Measurement of Coals, as the Lord Mayor, Recorder, and Board of Aldermen, or the Majority of them, shall think proper.

CHAP. X.

And Whereas it would be a great Relief and Advantage to the Journeymen, Tradesmen, and Manufacturers, and to the Poor of the City of Dublin, to establish a Repository, or Publick Coal Yard, or Coal Yards, for supplying them with Coals at moderate Prices; Be it Enacted by the Authority aforesaid, That One or more Yard or Yards shall be taken at the Expence of the Publick, for the Purpose of laying in a sufficient Quantity of Coals, for supplying the Journeymen, Tradesmen, and Manufacturers, and the Poor of the City of Dublin with Coals, in the Manner, and subject to the Regulations and Provisions herein after mentioned.

And be it Enacted by the Authority aforesaid, That the said Yard, or Yards, may be taken in such convenient Place or Places in the City of Dublin, as the Lord Mayor, Sheriffs, and Recorder of the said City, or any Three of them, shall appoint; and that the said Coals shall be bought in at the Publick Expence, when Coals are under Sixteen Shillings the Tun, and sold out, when Coals are sold at a higher Price than Eighteen Shillings the Tun; and the said Coals shall be sold out at a Profit of One Shilling the Tun, over and above the first Cost of the Coals at the Ship, and the Expence of Carriage from said Ship to the

the Publick Coal-Yard, to such Journey- CHAP.
men, Tradesmen, and Manufacturers, and to   X.
such Poor of the said City, as shall produce
Certificates from the Minister and Church-
Wardens of the respective Parishes, or from
the Lord Mayor, Recorder, or any Two
Aldermen of this City, setting forth the
Names, Trade, or Occupation of such Person, and the Street where he or she resides,
which Certificates the Director shall enter
upon a File or Files to be kept for that Purpose; and the Quantity of Half a Barrel,
and no more, shall be sold to any such Person in One Day.

And be it Enacted by the Authority aforesaid, That the Profits arising from the Sale
of the said Coals, shall be applied towards
paying the Yearly Rents of the said Yard or
Yards, and the Expences of carrying the
said Scheme into Execution.

And be it Enacted by the Authority aforesaid, That the Lord Lieutenant, or other
Chief Governor or Governors for the Time
being, shall appoint One discreet Person to
be Director or Superintendant of such Coal
Yard, or Coal Yards, which said Director
or Superintendant shall, from Time to
Time, buy Coals for supplying the said
Coal Yard, or Coal Yards, and shall give
a Draft upon His Majesty's Deputy Re-
D o 2   ceiver

CHAP. X.

ceiver General for the Amount of such Coals, as he shall from Time to Time buy for the Purpose of supplying the said Yard, or Yards, which said Draft shall be paid at the Treasury, and shall be allowed the Deputy Vice-Treasurer in his Accounts; and the said Director shall, once in every Month, pay into the Treasury such Sums of Money, as shall be paid into his Hands for the Sale of the said Coals, out of the said Yard or Yards.

Provided always, That the Sum so paid and advanced by the Deputy Vice-Treasurer, over and above the Sum so paid in to him by the said Director, shall not at any Time exceed in the Whole the Sum of Ten Thousand Pounds.

And be it Enacted by the Authority aforesaid, That the said Director shall be allowed the yearly Salary of Two Hundred Pounds, and shall have two Clerks under him, of his own Appointment, and for whom he shall be responsible, and that such Clerks shall be allowed the yearly Salary of Thirty Pounds each, for which said Salaries, the said Director, or Clerks, shall find Books, Paper, Pens and Ink, without making any Charge for the same to the Publick; and such Director, before he enters upon his said Office, shall be sworn

before

before the said Lord Mayor, which Oath he is hereby impowered to administer, faithfully and diligently to execute his said Office, and that he will, to the best of his Skill and Judgment, buy the said Coals at the most moderate Prices in his Power, and that he will not Waste or imbezzle any Part of the same, and that he will fairly Account for all such Sums as he shall receive by Sale of said Coals; and the said Director shall enter into a Bond, with two sufficient Securities, in the Penalty of Ten Thousand Pounds, conditioned for diligently and faithfully executing his said Office, and for accounting for such Sums of Money, as he shall from Time to Time receive, by Sale of the said Coals.

And be it Enacted by the Authority aforesaid, That the Lord Lieutenant, or other Chief Governor or Governors for the Time being, shall appoint one other discreet Person to be Comptroller of the Accounts and Conduct of the said Director, which said Comptroller shall have a Salary not exceeding One Hundred Pounds yearly, and shall examine and settle the Accounts of the said Director once in every Month, and shall once in every Fortnight at least inspect into, and carefully examine, the State and Condition of the said Coal-

CHAP. X. Yard, or Coal-Yards; and such Comptroller, before he enters upon his Office, shall be sworn before the Lord Mayor, which Oath the said Lord Mayor is hereby impowered to administer, faithfully, diligently, impartially, to execute his said Office of Comptroller, and shall, with two sufficient Sureties, enter into a Bond of the Penalty of Two Thousand Pounds, conditioned for his executing his said Office of Comptroller, faithfully, diligently, and impartially.

And be it Enacted by the Authority aforesaid, That the Lord Lieutenant, or other Chief Governor or Governors, and Privy Council, may be impowered to call the said Director, Comptroller and Clerks before them, and to inspect their Books, and to examine into their Conduct, and from Time to Time to remove them, or any of them, and to appoint other Persons in their Places; and the Lord Mayor of the said City is hereby impowered and required, once in every Month at the least, to inspect the said publick Coal-Yard, or Coal-Yards, and if he shall find that the same is not, or are not kept in a proper or regular Manner, to signify the same to the Lord Lieutenant, or other Chief Governor or Governors, and Privy Council.

And

CHAP. X.

And be it Enacted by the Authority aforesaid, That the said Director, once in every Month, shall lay before the said Lord Mayor and Board of Aldermen of the said City, his Books of Account for the said Month, which shall contain an exact Account of all Coals bought or sold by him, or his said Clerks, for one Month, antecedent to the Time of laying his said Books before them, and shall distinguish the Names of the Persons from and to Whom, and the respective Times When, and the Prices for Which the same were bought and sold, which said Accounts shall be verified by Affidavits, to be made by the said Director and his said Clerks; and the said Director shall, at the same Time, lay before the said Lord Mayor and Board of Aldermen, an Affidavit from the said Comptroller, that he believes the said Accounts have been kept for the said Month fairly and regularly, and that the said Director has, during the said Time, demeaned himself faithfully and diligently in his said Office (which said Affidavits shall be taken before the said Lord Mayor without Fee or Reward) and the said Lord Mayor and Board of Aldermen are hereby impowered, if they shall find it necessary, to examine such Director and his Clerks, and the said Comptroller, or any of them, upon Oath, touching

CHAP. X. touching the said Accounts, or the buying or selling of the said Coals, or in any respect touching the Execution of the said several Offices, or the Management of the said Coal-Yard, or Coal-Yards; and the said Lord Mayor, Recorder, and Board of Aldermen, or the Majority of them, if they find the said Accounts to be just and true, and approve of the Conduct of the said several Officers, are hereby required to sign their Names in the said Books at the End of the said Account; and if they in any respect disapprove of the said Accounts, or of the Conduct of any of the said Officers, they are hereby required to signify such their Disapprobation to the Lord Lieutenant, or other Chief Governor or Governors, and Privy Council.

And Whereas many Difficulties may arise in the Execution of this Scheme, that cannot now be foreseen; Be it Enacted by the Authority aforesaid, That the said Lord Mayor, Recorder, and Board of Aldermen, or the Majority of them, may make such Rules and By-Laws for the better managing and conducting the said Coal-Yard, and for the better Government of the said Director, Comptroller, and Clerks, as they shall find necessary, and that the same shall be as valid and effectual, as if the same were hereby Enacted.

Provided

Provided allways that the same shall, within one Month after they are made, be confirmed by the Lord Lieutenant, or Chief Governor or Governors, and Privy Council, and otherwise to be of no Force or Effect.

Provided also that the said By-Laws shall not be repugnant to any of the Directions given by this Act.

And be it Enacted by the Authority aforesaid, That all Penalties and Forfeitures to be recovered by this Act, shall be sued and recovered before the Recorder of the City of Dublin, in a Summary Way, by the Person who shall first sue for the same, in like Manner, and with the same Power of Appeal, as are directed by an Act of Parliament made in this Kingdom the Thirty-first Year of His late Majesty King George the Second, Intituled, An Act for the Recovery of small Debts, in a Summary Way, in the City of Dublin, and Liberties thereof, one Half to be paid to the Person who shall sue for the same, the other Half to be paid to the said Director, towards increasing the Fund for carrying the said Scheme into Execution.

CHAP. X. And be it Enacted by the Authority aforesaid, That this Act shall continue in Force for Two Years, from the twenty-fifth Day of March, in the Year One thousand seven hundred and sixty-two, and from thence to the End of the then next Session of Parliament.

AN ACT

TO

Prevent Abuses committed by Justices of Peace, acting under the Charters of Cities and Towns Corporate.

DUBLIN:

Printed by BOULTER GRIERSON, Printer to the King's most Excellent Majesty. MDCCLXII.

(157)

AN ACT

TO

Prevent Abuses committed by Justices of Peace, acting under the Charters of Cities and Towns Corporate.

CHAP. XI.

WHEREAS it frequently happens, That great Abuses are committed by Justices of Peace, acting under the Charters of Cities and Towns Corporate, and notwithstanding such Abuses, it may

Chap. XI.
may be a Doubt whether such Justices of the Peace, so offending, are, or may be removable from their Offices, or the Execution thereof, by any Law now in being; For Remedy whereof, Be it Enacted by the King's Most Excellent Majesty, by and with the Advice and Consent of the Lords Spiritual and Temporal, and Commons in this present Parliament Assembled, and by the Authority of the same, That if any such Justice shall wilfully commit any Offence, contrary to his Duty as a Justice of Peace, every such Justice, shall, upon Conviction of such Offence, on an Information to be filed in the Court of King's Bench, be for ever disabled to act as a Justice of the Peace, for or within such City or Town-Corporate, in Case the Court or Judge, before whom such Information shall be tryed, shall, in open Court, before the same is adjourned, certify under his or their Hand or Hands, that he or they is or are satisfied with the Verdict given upon such Information.

And be it further Enacted by the Authority aforesaid, That the Tryal of all such Informations shall be had in some indifferent County, to be appointed by the Court of King's Bench.

Provided

Provided allways, That nothing in this Act contained, shall extend to Justices of the Peace, who are or shall hereafter be appointed by Virtue of any Commission of the Peace, issued, or to be issued by His Majesty, His Heirs and Successors.

CHAP. XI.

CHAP. XII.

AN ACT

FOR

The Security of

PROTESTANT PURCHASERS.

DUBLIN:
Printed by BOULTER GRIERSON, Printer to the King's
Most Excellent Majesty. MDCCLXII.

AN ACT FOR

The Security of

PROTESTANT PURCHASERS.

CHAP. XII.

FOR the Relief and Security of Protestant Purchasers, Be it Enacted by the King's Most Excellent Majesty, by and with the Advice and Consent of the Lords Spiritual and Temporal,

and

CHAP. XII.

and Commons in this present Parliament assembled, and by the Authority of the same, That no Sale for a full and valuable Consideration of any Manors, Messuages, Lands, Tenements, or Hereditaments, or of any Estate or Interest therein, by any Person or Persons being reputed Owner or Owners, or in the Possession or Receipt of the Rents and Profits thereof, heretofore made to or for any Protestant Purchaser or Purchasers, and merely and only for the Benefit of a Protestant or Protestants, shall be impeached or avoided, for, or by Reason, or upon Pretence of any of the Disabilities, Incapacities, or Forfeitures imposed or mentioned in or by the Acts of Parliament made to prevent the further Growth of Popery, or any of them, or in or by an Act of Parliament passed in this Kingdom, in the Nineteenth Year of His late Majesty King George the Second, Intituled, An Act for the more effectual preventing His Majesty's Subjects from entering into foreign Service, and for publishing an Act of the Seventh Year of King William the Third, Intituled, An Act to prevent foreign Education, nor shall the Manors, Messuages, Lands, Tenements, or Hereditaments, or the Estate or Interest therein, so sold, be sued for or recovered under the said Acts of Parliament, or any of them.

Provided

CHAP. XII.

Provided that nothing herein contained shall extend to, or affect, or be construed to affect, any Judgment or Decree obtained, or any Suit at Law or in Equity, instituted on or before the Second Day of March, One thousand seven hundred and sixty-two, for the Recovery of such Manors, Messuages, Lands, Tenements, or Hereditaments, or such Estate or Interest therein.

CHAP.
XIII.

AN ACT

FOR

Quieting the Possessions of Protestants, deriving under Converts from the Popish Religion.

DUBLIN:

Printed by BOULTER GRIERSON, Printer to the King's most Excellent Majesty. MDCCLXII.

AN ACT

FOR

Quieting the Possessions of Protestants, deriving under Converts from the Popish Religion.

CHAP. XIII.

Whereas many Convertts from the Popish to the Protestant Religion, as by Law Established, have neglected strictly to perform the legal Requisites of Conformity, by Means whereof, many Protestant Purchasers, and others, deriving under such Convertts, may be affected: For Remedy whereof, Be it Enacted by the King's Most Excellent Majesty, by and with the Advice and Consent of the Lords

CHAP. XIII.

Lords Spiritual and Temporal, and Commons in this present Parliament assembled, and by the Authority of the same, That the Title of any Protestant to any Estate or Interest in any Lands, Tenements, or Hereditaments, heretofore derived from, or under any Convert, by Purchase, or otherwise, shall not be impeached, or in any wise affected, by Reason or Means of any Omission or Neglect of such Convert, in performing the Legal Requisites of Conformity; Provided such Convert did obtain the Bishop's Certificate of his or her Conformity, and from and after the obtaining of the same, professed the Protestant Religion, and was, and continued a Protestant.

And be it further Enacted by the Authority aforesaid, That all such Persons as have heretofore obtained the Bishop's Certificate of their Conformity, and from and after the obtaining of the same, have professed the Protestant Religion, and have continued Protestants, and have not performed all the other Legal Requisites of Conformity, and shall perform the same before the Twenty fifth Day of March, One thousand seven hundred and sixty three, shall, from the Time of his having filed the Bishop's Certificate, of his or her Conformity from the Popish to the Protestant Religion,

Religion, be deemed, and taken to be, Protestants of the Established Church, to all Intents and Purposes.

Provided always, That nothing herein contained, shall impeach, or in any Wise affect any Judgment or Decree, made or given in any Court of Law or Equity, or any Action or Suit, commenced before the Twenty fifth Day of March, One thousand seven hundred and sixty two, and now depending; but that all such Judgments and Decrees shall remain, and be in such like Force, and all such Actions and Suits shall and may be prosecuted in such Manner, as if this Act had not been made; any Thing herein contained to the contrary notwithstanding.

CHAP. XIV.

AN ACT

FOR

Preventing Frauds and Abuses in the vending, preparing, and administring Drugs and Medicines.

DUBLIN:
Printed by BOULTER GRIERSON, Printer to the King's Most Excellent Majesty. MDCCLXII.

AN ACT FOR

Preventing Frauds and Abuses in the vending, preparing, and administring Drugs and Medicines.

CHAP. XIV.

WHEREAS many most dangerous and destructive Frauds and Abuses are daily committed in the vending, preparing, and administring of Drugs and Medicines: For Remedy whereof, Be it

CHAP. XIV.

Be it Enacted by the King's Most Excellent Majesty, by and with the Advice and Consent of the Lords Spiritual and Temporal, and Commons in this present Parliament assembled, and by the Authority of the same, That from and after the First Day of May, in the Year of our Lord, One thousand seven hundred and sixty-two, the Presidents, Censors, and Fellows of the King and Queen's College of Physicians, Ireland, shall have full Power and Authority to enlarge the Number of their Body, by admitting into the Fellowship of their Body such and so many other learned and worthy Doctors of Physick, as the said President, Censors, and Fellows of the said College of Physicians shall, from Time to Time, judge neccessary and fit to be admitted, upon due Examination, by Election of the said College of Physicians.

And be it further Enacted by the Authority aforesaid, That the said President, Censors, and Fellows of the said College of Physicians, may have full Power and Authority to elect and appoint four of the Fellows, or Members of their Body, to be Inspectors and Examiners of all Elaboratories, Shops, Ware or Store-Houses, Cellars, Vaults, Room or Rooms, and of all other Repositories of what Kind or Name

Name soever they may be, in the House or Houses, or other Place or Places belonging to any Apothecary, Chemist, or Druggist, or other Person or Persons whatsoever, who now do, or hereafter shall import for Sale, or buy and sell, or keep for that Purpose, or who prepare, administer, or sell, or keep for those Purposes, any Drug, or Simple or Compound Medicine, of what Nature or Denomination soever, which is or may be used as Medicine for the Health of Man's Body, within the City of Dublin, and Ten Miles Circuit thereof.

And be it further Enacted by the Authority aforesaid, That the said College of Physicians shall, within three Days after electing the Inspectors or Examiners aforesaid, give Notice in Writing to the Master and Wardens of the Corporation of Apothecaries of the City of Dublin, that the said College has chosen Four of its Members, as Inspectors and Examiners of Drugs and Medicines, pursuant to this Act, and requiring the said Corporation to elect and appoint Two of the most skilful and honest Apothecaries of their said Corporation as Assistants to the said Examiners, and to return their Names, and Places of Abode, to the said College of Physicians, within Three Days after such Notice shall be given in Writing, as aforesaid,

CHAP. said, Which said Election, or Appointment
XIV. of Two Assistant Apothecaries, shall nevertheless, be subjected to be excepted against, or approved of, by the said College of Physicians; and that Whensoever the said College of Physicians shall object to the Return of both, or either of the Assistant Apothecaries, made to them as aforesaid, the said Corporation of Apothecaries shall be obliged, upon Notice from the said College of Physicians, as aforesaid, to come to a new Election and Nomination, and to make a new Return, as aforesaid, in the Room of both, or either of the Persons, so disapproved of by the said College of Physicians.

Provided always, and be it further Enacted by the Authority aforesaid, That if the said Corporation of Apothecaries should neglect to elect, appoint, or return such Assistant Apothecaries; or in case the said elected, appointed, or returned, or Assistant Apothecaries, should refuse or neglect to come to the said Physicians, upon due Notice, as aforesaid, it may and shall be lawful for the said Examining Physicians, to proceed without them.

And be it further Enacted by the Authority aforesaid, That the Four Physicians, appointed by the said College of Physicians,

CHAP. XIV.

as aforesaid, shall be the Visitors, Inspectors, and Examiners of the Shops, Ware-houses, Store-houses, Elaboratories, Rooms, Cellars, Vaults, or other Places or Repositories, where Drugs, or Simple or Compound Medicines, of any Denomination or Kind whatsoever, are made, prepared, administered, or exposed to Sale, or kept for that Purpose; and the Examiners of all such Drugs and Medicines as shall be found therein, within the City of Dublin, or Liberties thereof, or within Ten Miles Circuit thereof; and that the said Two Apothecaries returned by the Corporation of Apothecaries, and approved of by the said College of Physicians, shall be Assistants to the said Four Physicians, in the Execution of the Powers herein after granted by this Act, which said Four Inspectors and Examiners, with the said Two Assistant Apothecaries, shall serve for One Year only, and not to be liable to be appointed again for Three Years after, without their own Consent.

And be it further Enacted by the Authority aforesaid, That it may and shall be lawful for the said President, Censors, and Fellows of the said College of Physicians, to summon before them the Four Fellows, or other Members of their Body, appointed Inspectors and Examiners, as aforesaid, and

Chap. XIV. and the said Two Apothecaries, appointed Assistants as aforesaid, and to administer to each and every of them, the following Oath:

I *A. B.* do solemnly and sincerely promise and swear, that I will, to the best of my Knowledge, Skill, and Judgment, without Hatred or Evil Will, without Partiality, Affection, Favour, or Fear, justly, equally, and faithfully discharge the Trust, and execute the Powers vested in me by an Act, Intituled, *An Act for Preventing Frauds and Abuses in the Vending, Preparing, and Administring Drugs and Medicines.*

So help me God.

And be it further Enacted by the Authority aforesaid, That the said Examiners, or any Two of them, with the said Assistant Apothecaries, or one of them, shall have full Power and Authority, and are hereby required, four Times at least in the Year, or oftner, if they shall see Occasion, in the Day-time, to enter and inspect all and every Shop, Ware or Store-house, Cellar, Vault, Room or Rooms, Elaboratories, or other Reposotories, of what Kind or Denomination soever, appertaining to Apothecaries, Chemists, Druggists, or other Person or Persons Whatsoever, who now do, or hereafter shall buy and sell, expose to sale, or keep for that Purpose, any Manner of Drugs, simple or compound Medicines, used,

used, or to be used for Medicines for the Health of Man's Body, and therein strictly to search for, and fully and fairly to examine the Nature and Quality of all and every Kind of Drug, Simple or Compound Medicine, or Chemical Preparation, used, or to be used for Medicine as aforesaid.

And in Case the said Examiners shall find, in such Search and Inspection, any Kind of Drug, Simple or Compound Medicine, or Chemical Preparation, which, to the best of their Judgments, shall appear unsound, corrupt, adulterated, or unfaithfully, dishonestly, or unskilfully compounded, or otherwise prepared, so as to be rendered unwholesome or unfit to be used as Medicine for the Health of Man's Body, all and every Drug and Medicine by the said Examiners adjudged corrupt or Defective, as aforesaid, to condemn and seize upon, and see burned, or otherwise totally destroyed, by the Hands of the Beadle of the said College of Physicians, or any other Person or Persons, by the Examiners for the Time being, appointed for that Purpose.

Provided nevertheless, and be it further Enacted by the Authority aforesaid, That in case the said Examiners, or the Major Part of them, shall condemn any Drugs or Medicines, as unfit to be administred or used in

Medicine for the Health of Man's Body, and that the Owner or Owners, Possessor or Possessors of such Drugs or Medicines, or in his Absence the Person having the Custody or chief Care thereof, shall, before the burning or destroying thereof, insist that the same ought not to be burned or destroyed, and shall forthwith, by Writing under his or their Hands, appeal to, and desire the Judgment of the President, Censors, and Fellows of the said College of Physicians in Dublin, for the Time being, thereupon, then, and in such Case, the said Examiners shall cause the said Drugs or Medicines, so seized, to be Weighed, and with the Boxes, Pots, Glasses, or other Vessels containing the same, and the Reasons, in Writing, for condemning thereof, subscribed by each of the said Examiners condemning the same, to be then and there put into a Box, and sealed with their respective Seals of each of the said Examiners, and the Seal of the Person or Persons so insisting, if such Person or Persons shall think fit to put his or their Seal thereto, which Box, so sealed, the Examiners for the Time being, shall commit to the Care and Custody of the Beadle of the said College of Physicians, where it shall remain for any Time, not exceeding Fourteen Days, within which Time the President of the College of Physicians shall summon an Assembly, or Meeting of the Censors, and other Fellows

Fellows and Members of their College or Body, in the usual Manner of summoning such Meetings or Assemblies, Whereof the Owner or Possessor of the said condemned Drugs and Medicines, shall have four Days Notice in Writing, to be given or left, to or for the Person or Persons, by or for whom such Appeal was made, at the Place Where the condemned Drugs or Medicines were found, that he or they may attend the said Meeting, if he or they shall think fit; and that the President, Censors, and Fellows, so assembled, shall have Power and Authority, being no less in Number than Five, exclusive of the said Examiners, to open such Box, from Time to Time, in the Presence of the Person or Persons, by, or for whom such Appeal was made, if he or they shall there appear; and in Default of their Appearance (due Notice being given as aforesaid) then, without him or them, and to proceed to examine, and finally determine concerning such Drugs and Medicines, as aforesaid, contained therein; And if the said President and Assembly, being not less in Number than as aforesaid, or the major Part thereof, confirm and ratify the Judgment of the said Examiners, then the said Examiners, for the Time being, shall cause all such Drugs and Medicines, as aforesaid, so condemned, and Vessels containing the same, to be pub-lickly

Chap. XIV. lickly burned, or otherwise destroyed, before the Doors of the Person or Persons in whose Shop, Elaboratory, Ware-house, or Room, the same were found, in such Manner, and at such Time, as the said Examiners, for the Time being, shall think fit and direct: Provided the said President, Censors, and Fellows, shall first take the Oath herein before prescribed, Which the President is hereby required to take, and impowered and required to administer.

Provided allways, and be it further Enacted by the Authority aforesaid, That if, or in case the Drugs or Medicines seized by the Examiners, shall not be condemned within fourteen Days, by the said Assembly of President, Censors, and Fellows, or shall be deemed sound and good, and meet to be administered as Medicines for the Health of Man's Body, that then, the said Drugs and Medicines shall be immediately returned to the Owner, together with the Boxes, Pots, Glasses, or other Vessels wherein the same are contained, safe, and in good Condition, without Waste or other Damage Whatsoever.

And be it further Enacted by the Authority aforesaid, That in case any Apothecary, Chemist, Druggist, or other Person or Persons

CHAP. XIV.

sons who now do, or hereafter shall, buy and sell, expose to Sale, or keep for that purpose, any Drug, Simple or Compound Medicine, or Chemical Preparation, used, or to be used for Medicine, shall presume to obstruct, let, or molest the said Examiners, or their Assistant or Assistants, Beadle or Beadles, or other Servant or Servants, in the Execution of this Act, or any Part thereof, that every such Offender in this Case, shall forfeit for every such Offence, the Sum of Twenty Pounds.

And for the better ascertaining the Nature and Qualities, and the Doses, and Uses of all Drugs, Simple and Compound Medicines, and Chemical Preparations, Be it further Enacted by the Authority aforesaid, That it may be lawful for the said President, Censors, and Fellows of the College of Physicians, for the Time being, to frame and publish a Code, or Pharmacopœia, containing a Catalogue of such Drugs, or Simple Medicines, as they shall judge necessary for the Prescriptions or Uses of Physicians and Chirurgeons, together with Forms and Rules for preparing and compounding the same, Chemically and Galenically, as they shall judge fit and necessary for the Practice of Physick and Chirurgery, directing not only the Form and Manner, but the various Vessels, and other

A a a   Utensils,

CHAP. XIV. Utenfils, and the Materials of which such Veſſels or Utenſils ſhall be respectively made or compoſed, as alſo the Meaſures, Weights and Scales, by which all ſuch Medicinal Drugs, Preparations, and Compoſitions ſhall be difpenfed and fold, which faid Code or Pharmacopoeia, ſhall be followed and obſerved by all and every Apothecary, Chemiſt, Druggiſt, and other Perſon or Perſons, who now do, or hereafter ſhall prepare, adminiſter, ſell, expoſe to Sale, or keep for that Purpoſe, any Kind of Drug, Simple or Compound Medicine, or Chemical, or other Medicinal Preparation whatſoever, throughout this Kingdom.

And be it further Enacted by the Authority aforeſaid, That if any Apothecary, Chemiſt, or Druggiſt, or other Perſon or Perſons, who now do, or hereafter ſhall, make, prepare, compound, ſell, expoſe to Sale, or keep for that Purpoſe, any Kind of Drug, or Medicinal Preparation, or Compound whatſoever, ſhall preſume to make, prepare, compound, difpenfe, or fell any other Officinal Preparations or Compoſitions, or make up any extemporaneous Preſcription of any Phyſician or Chirurgeon in this Kingdom, by any other Form or Rule, in any other Utenſils, or by any other

other Measures or Weights, than shall be so directed and appointed by the said College of Physicians, such Offender shall forfeit and pay, for every such Offence, the Sum of Ten Pounds, Sterling, unless where the contrary is, or shall be directed by some Regular Practitioner, and that for his own private Use solely.

CHAP. XIV.

And be it further Enacted by the Authority aforesaid, That the aforesaid Examiners, may and shall examine the several Utensils, Measures, Scales and Weights, in all and every Place or Places, where any Kind of Drugs or Medicinal Preparations or Compounds are sold, prepared, or compounded, for Sale, exposed to Sale, or kept for that Purpose, and seize or destroy all such Utensils, Measures, Weights and Scales, as they shall find, contrary to the Rules or Directions of the said Code, or Pharmacopoeia, or otherwise defective, or unlawful, saving to the Delinquent the Benefit of an Appeal to the College of Physicians, as in the Case of condemned Drugs or Medicines, as aforesaid.

Provided nevertheless, That this Act, or any Part thereof, shall not be construed to extend to any Merchant Adventurer, who shall import Simple Drugs, or Medi-

CHAP.
XIV.

cines for Sale, and does not prepare, compound, or retail the same.

And for the better preventing and punishing Frauds and Abuses in the preparing, compounding, and vending of Drugs and Medicines, in the more remote Parts of this Kingdom; Be it Enacted by the Authority aforesaid, That it may and shall be lawful for the Chief Magistrate of every City, Borough, or Town-Corporate, for the Time being, unless he or they happen to follow the Art, Business, or Occupation of an Apothecary, Chemist, or Druggist, in all or any of their Branches, and then, for the Sheriffs of any City, or any Two Justices of the Peace of any City, or for any Two Justices of the Peace of a County, who live nearest to any Borough, or any Town, whose Chief Magistrate happens to follow the Art, Business, or Occupation of an Apothecary, Chemist, or Druggist, or in the Towns where no Magistrate resides, to summon any Two or more Doctors of Physick, Graduates of Oxford, Cambridge, Edinburgh, or of any other University of Great Britain, Leyden, or Dublin, or Licentiates of the King and Queen's College of Physicians in Ireland, and to administer to each and every of them, the Examiner's Oath, herein before mentioned; Which Physicians, so summoned or sworn, being no less than Two

Two in Number, with the Chief Magi- CHAP.
strate of the City, or Town, shall have XIV.
full Power and Authority to search and
inspect all and every Shop, Store or Ware-
house, Elaboratory, or other Repository of all
and every Apothecary, Chemist, and Druggist, and of all and every Person or Persons
who now do, or hereafter shall prepare, compound for Sale, sell, expose to Sale, or keep
for that Purpose, any Kind of Drug, Simple
or Compound Medicine, Chemical or other
Preparation, used, or to be used for Medicine, and to examine all such Drugs and
Medicines, together with all the Utensils,
Measures, Scales and Weights, and to
seize and destroy all such Drugs and Medicines, Utensils, Measures, Scales and
Weights, as they shall find, and adjudge
unsound, adulterate, corrupt, unwholsome,
defective, or otherwise unlawful; saving,
nevertheless, to the Party, the Benefit of
an Appeal to the College of Physicians in
Dublin.

And in case the Owner of any Drug
or Medicine, or the Person acting for him,
in his Absence, shall appeal to the College
of Physicians, Be it Enacted by the Authority aforesaid, That a Sample or Samples
of the Drug or Medicine, so condemned,
under the Seal of the Examiners, as well
as the Owner or Owners, if he or they
shall

CHAP. XIV.

shall think proper, be sent with all convenient Speed, by the Chief Magistrate present at such Examination and Condemnation, to the College of Physicians in Dublin, who shall be fully impowered and authorized finally to determine the same. And in case the said College of Physicians shall confirm the Judgment of the said Examiners, it may and shall be lawful for the Chief Magistrate to burn, or otherwise destroy, the rest and Residue of the Drugs and Medicines so seized, at the Offender's Door, upon a Market-Day, and also to oblige the said Offender to pay for the Carriage of the said Sample or Samples, and Appeal to the College of Physicians, any Sum, not exceeding Forty Shillings: But in case the said College of Physicians shall not affirm the Judgment of the said Examiners, on the Condemnation of any Drug or Medicine, then, within Twenty four Hours after the Judgment of the College of Physicians shall be known, the Chief Magistrate shall publickly restore the Drugs and Medicines, so condemned and seized, without Waste or other Damage.

And to the Intent that Marks may be set upon all and every Person or Persons offending in the preparing, administring, vending, importing, exposing to Sale, or keeping

keeping for that Purpose, for the Satisfaction and Safety, as well of those who have Occasion to consume, as of those who prescribe Medicines.

Be it further Enacted by the Authority aforesaid, That the several Examiners, appointed by this Act, may, and shall make due Returns after every Exercise of the Powers vested in them by this Act, to the President, Censors, and Fellows of the College of Physicians in Dublin, setting forth the Name and Place of Abode of every Apothecary, Chemist, Druggist, or other Person whose Shop, Elaboratory, Store or Ware-House, or other Repository, they have visited and examined, together with the State and Condition of the Drugs and Medicines in all and every such Shop, Elaboratory, Ware or Store-House, or other Repository, and how the same are furnished, as well with Drugs and Medicines, as with fit Utensils and lawful Measures, Scales and Weights, as also the State and Condition of such Drugs and Medicines, as they have been called to examine in the Hands of Importers or Merchants.

And whereas many fraudulent and unskilful Apothecaries, Chemists, or Druggists, daily presume to sell one Drug or Medicine

CHAP. VIV. Medicine for another, as well as to omit sundry Ingredients in Shop Compositions and extemporaneous Prescriptions, or to substitute one Drug or Medicine for another, to the great Detriment of the Buyers or Patient, as well as the Prescriber.

For Remedy whereof, Be it Enacted by the Authority aforesaid, That no Apothecary, Chemist, Druggist, or other Person or Persons whatsoever, who now do, or hereafter shall prepare or compound, sell or expose to Sale, or keep for that Purpose any simple or compound Medicine, Chemical, or other medicinal Preparation whatsoever, shall from and after the Commencement of this Act, sell any Drug or Medicine in the Place or Stead of another, without informing the Buyer thereof of the Charge, and the Reason or Necessity for so doing, giving the same in Writing if demanded.

And that no Apothecary, Chemist, Druggist, or other Person or Persons who now do, or hereafter shall prepare, dispense or compound, sell, expose to Sale, or keep for that Purpose any Drug or Medicine whatsoever, shall presume to substitute any one Ingredient for another, or to omit or leave out any one Ingredient in any Officinal, or other Composition, or extemporaneous

extemporaneous Prescription, without the Approbation or Leave of the College of Physicians in Dublin, or of the immediate Prescribers of such Composition, or extemporaneous Prescription, in Dublin, or elsewhere, or without signifying on the Cover or Label of such Medicine, the Omission, or Substitute, and the Reason or Necessity for making the same, under the Penalty of Forty Shillings Sterling, for every such Imposition, Omission, or Substitute, proved by the Confession of the Party, or by the Oath of one or more credible Witnesses, before the Chief Magistrate of the Town where such Offence shall be committed, or before the next Justices of the Peace, or going Judge of Assize, where no other Civil Magistrate shall happen to be resident. And in order to prevent the Incertainties and Dangers which may attend the setting down the Quantities of Medicines in Chemical and Numeral Characters in Prescriptions, Be it Enacted by the Authority aforesaid, That every Physician, Chirurgeon, or other Person or Persons who now do, or hereafter shall take upon him or them to prescribe internal or external Remedies for the Health of Man's Body in this Kingdom, shall hereafter write, or set down the Quantity or Quantities of all and every Medicine or Ingredient, whether simple or compound, which

C c c   be

CHAP. XIV.

he or they shall prescribe in any Recipe, Formula, or Prescription, in Words at length, and not in Chemical or Numeral Characters, under the Penalty of Forty Shillings for every such Omission.

And be it further Enacted by the Authority aforesaid, That all and every Physician, Chirurgeon, or other Person or Persons taking upon him or them to prescribe Medicines, whether for internal or external Use, or Application for the Health of Man's Body, shall subscribe every such Prescription with his Name or Surname, or the Initial Letters of his Name and Surname, and with those also of his Profession, whether Physician or Chirurgeon, and if a Physician, with the Name, or the Initial Letter of the Name of the University or Universities of which he is a Doctor, or other Graduate in Physick, under the Penalty of Forty Shillings for every Omission, unless he be a Member of the Royal College of Physicians, in which Case the Initial Letters of his Name alone may be sufficient.

And in order to prevent the dangerous and destructive Practice of the promiscuous keeping, handling, preparing and vending sundry deletery or noxious Drugs, not safely used, or to be used as Medicines,

CHAP. XIV.

cines, Be it Enacted by the Authority aforesaid, That from and after the Commencement of this Act, no Apothecary, Chemist, Druggist, or other Person or Persons whatsoever, who now do, or hereafter shall prepare, administer or sell, expose to Sale, or keep for that Purpose any Drugs, simple or compound Medicines, or Chemical or other Preparations used, or to be used for Medicine, shall keep, handle, powder, or otherwise prepare, weigh, measure, or sell, expose to Sale, or keep for that Purpose any Arsenick, whether White or yellow Arsenick, or Orpiment, or red Arsenick, or Realgar, or any other arsenical Preparation or Composition in the same Shop, Elaboratory, Ware, or Store-House, Cellar, Vault, Room or Rooms, or other Place or Places, or Repositories of what Denomination or Kind whatsoever, or in any Morter, Measure, or Scales, where any Drug, simple or compound Medicine, Chemical, or other Preparation used, or to be used, as Medicines for the Health of Man's Body, are kept, handled, dispensed, powdered, prepared, measured, weighed, sold, exposed to Sale, or kept for these Purposes, under the Penalty of Five Pounds for every such Offence, or Repetition or Continuance of such Offence.

CHAP. XIV. And for the better preventing the dangerous and destructive Practice of tinselling or covering, or otherwise disguising Electuaries, Bolus, Pills, or other Medicines, with unwholsome Metallick Leaves, or Powders; Be it Enacted by the Authority aforesaid, That no Apothecary, Chemist, Druggist, or other Person or Persons who now do, or hereafter shall prepare, administer, sell, or expose to Sale, or keep for that Purpose any Drugs, simple or compound Medicine, Chemical, or other medicinal Preparation, shall henceforth presume to tinsel over, cover, or otherwise disguise, or mix with any Electuary, Bolus, Pill, Powder, or other Drug or Medicine, any Leaves, Powders, or other Preparations of Copper or Brass, called Dutch Metal, Dutch Leaves, or Dutch Gold, or under Whatsoever Denomination they may be known or called, under the Penalty of Forty Shillings Sterling for every such Offence.

And be it further Enacted by the Authority aforesaid, That all the Penalties inflicted by this Act, may be sued for and recovered in a Summary Way, before the Lord Mayor and Recorder of the City of Dublin, or the Mayor, or other Chief Magistrate, and Recorder of any other City

City or Town Corporate, where such Offences are or shall be committed, who are hereby impowered and authorized to hear and determine the same, and to levy such Penalties by Distress and Sale of the Offender's Goods, returning the Overplus to the Owner (if any be) the Charges of taking and disposing of the Goods so distrained, being first deducted, one Moiety of which said Penalties, when recovered, shall be applied by the College of Physicians in Dublin, and by the Chief Magistrate and Examining Physicians in other Cities and Towns Corporate, for the purchasing Medicines for the Use of the Poor, and the other Moiety thereof for the Use of the Informer.

Provided always, and be it further Enacted by the Authority aforesaid, That if any Person or Persons shall at any Time be sued or prosecuted for putting in Execution any Power or Authority given by this Act, or any Part thereof, such Person or Persons shall, or may plead the General Issue, and give this Act, and the special Matter in Evidence.

And be it further Enacted by the Authority aforesaid, That this Act shall be deemed and taken, and is hereby declared to be a publick Act to all Intents and
D d d   Purposes,

CHAP. XIV. Purposes, and shall be judicially taken notice of, and allowed as such in all Courts within this Kingdom, by all Judges and Justices whatsoever, without specially pleading the same, and that this present Act shall continue in Force for the Term of Three Years, and from thence to the End of the then next Session of Parliament, and no longer.

AN

CHAP. XV.

AN ACT

FOR

Altering and Amending an Act of Parliament passed in the Seventh Year of the Reign of His late Majesty King *George* the Second, Intituled, *An Act for Repairing the Road leading from the Bridge over the Bann-Water, commonly called the* Bann-Bridge, *in the County of* Down, *to the Town of* Belfast, *in the County of* Antrim.

DUBLIN:
Printed by BOULTER GRIERSON, Printer to the King's Most Excellent Majesty. MDCCLXII.

AN ACT

FOR

Altering and Amending an Act of Parliament passed in the Seventh Year of the Reign of His late Majesty King *George* the Second, Intituled, *An Act for Repairing the Road leading from the Bridge over the* Bann-Water, *commonly called the* Bann-Bridge, *in the County of* Down, *to the Town of* Belfast, *in the County of* Antrim.

CHAP. XV.

WHEREAS pursuant to an Act of Parliament passed in the Seventh Year of the Reign of his late Majesty King George the Second, Intituled, An Act for repairing the Road leading from the Bridge over the *Bann-Water*, commonly

monly called the *Bann-Bridge*, in the County of *Down*, to the Town of *Belfast*, in the County of *Antrim*, the Trustees, in the said Act named, have borrowed the Sum of Four Thousand, Nine Hundred and Twenty Pounds, Sterling, and have applied the same to the Uses directed by the said Act; but it hath been found by Experience, that the Tolls levied pursuant to the said Act, are not sufficient to discharge the Interest of the Principal Money so borrowed, and to keep the said Road in Repair, and answer the other necessary Expences attending the Execution of, and intended to be provided for, by the said Act. Neither, by Reason of some Defects in the said Act, have the said Trustees been able to enforce the Application of the Two Days Parish Labour, appropriated thereby to the Repair of the said Road, insomuch that a considerable Arrear of Interest is now due upon the said Money, and the said Road is now greatly out of Repair, and also several of the Gates erected thereon for collecting the Tolls, pursuant to the said Act, have, by unknown Persons riotously assembled, been pulled down and destroyed; by all which Means, and the shortness of the Term in the said Act mentioned, for the Continuance thereof, and the great Length of the said Road, which renders it inconvenient for the Trustees, who live near the different Parts thereof,

to

Georgii Tertii Regis. 203

CHAP. XV.

to assemble together, there is great Danger that the End, by the said Act proposed, of putting and keeping the said Road in proper Repair, may be disappointed, and also that the several Persons who have lent their Money on the Credit and Security of the said Act, may lose the same.

For Remedy thereof, Be it Enacted by the King's Most Excellent Majesty, by and with the Advice and Consent of the Lords Spiritual and Temporal, and Commons in this present Parliament assembled, and by the Authority of the same, That from and after the First Day of May next, instead of the Tolls and Duties at present payable on the said Road, the following shall be received and taken (that is to say) for every Coach, Berlin, Chariot, Calash, Chaise, or Chair, if drawn by six Horses, or other Cattle of any Kind, the Sum of One Shilling and Six Pence, and if drawn by any less Number of such Cattle than Six, and more than Two, then the Sum of One Shilling, but if drawn by Two only of such Cattle, then the Sum of Six Pence; for every Waggon, Wain, Cart, or Carriage with Four Wheels, the Sum of Ten Shillings; for every Wain, Cart, or Carriage with Two Wheels, drawn by more than Two Horses, or other Cattle of any Kind, the Sum of Two

E e e 2   Shillings

CHAP.
XV.

Shillings and Six Pence; for every Cart, or other Carriage, drawn by One or Two Horses, or other Cattle, the Sum of Four Pence; for every Carriage, commonly called Chair or Chaise, drawn by One Horse, or other Beast, the Sum of Three Pence; for every Cat, or other such Carriage, drawn by One Horse, or other Beast, the Sum of One Penny Halfpenny, except Carrs loaden with Turf, and for each of them One Penny; and for every Horse, or other Beast, loaden with Turf, and not drawing, One Halfpenny; for every other Horse, Mare, Gelding, Mule, or Ass, laden or unladen, and not drawing, One Penny; for every Drove of Oxen, or other neat Cattle, the Sum of One Shilling and Eight Pence by the Score, and so in Proportion for any greater or lesser Number; for every Drove of Calves, Swine, Sheep, or Lambs, the Sum of Five Pence by the Score, and so in Proportion for any greater or lesser Number.

Provided nevertheless, That beside the Exemptions from Tolls, in the said former Act mentioned, for every Cart drawn by One Horse, passing or travelling on the said Road, the Tire of the Wheels of which shall exceed Three Inches in Breadth at the Sole thereof, and be put on with broad or rose-headed Nails, no more than Half

Georgii Tertii Regis.

Half of the Tolls before mentioned, shall be paid; and that all Waggons, Carts, Carrs, or Carriages, with Two or with Four Wheels, and drawn by any Number of Horses whatsoever, shall be exempted and excused from paying any of the said Tolls, provided the Tire of the said Wheels shall exceed seven Inches in the Breadth thereof; any Thing in this, or the said former Act, to the contrary notwithstanding.

And be it further Enacted by the Authority aforesaid, That from and after the Time aforesaid, the Governor, and the Custos Rotulorum of the County of Down; the Governor and Custos Rotulorum of the County of Antrim; the Right Reverend the Lord Bishops of Down and Connor, and of Dromore; the Knights of the Shire for the Counties of Down and Antrim, and the Burgesses in Parliament for the Boroughs of Hillsborough, in the County of Down, and Lisburn and Belfast, in the County of Antrim; the Lords of the Manors of Gill-Hall, Dromore, Hillsborough, Castlereagh, Slatueils, Drumbracklin and Holywood, in the County of Down; and of Kilultagh and Belfast, in the County of Antrim; the Justices of the Peace for the Counties of Down and Antrim, respectively; the Dean of Dromore, the Archdeacon of Down, and his resident Curates at Hillsborough, Drumbo and Drumbeg, all in

Chap. XV. the County of Down respectively; the Rectors of the Parishes of Dromore, and of Knock and Bredagh, in the County of Down; and of Lisburn, in the County of Antrim, and the resident Curate of each of them; the Vicar of the Parish of Shankill, otherwise Belfast, in the County of Antrim, and his resident Curate; and the Vicar of the Parish of Seapatrick, in the County of Down, and his resident Curate; the several Seneschals of the said Manors of Gill-Hall, Dromore, Hillsborough, Castlereagh, Slatueils, Drumbracklin, Holywood, Kilultagh and Belfast, and the Sovereigns of Hillsborough and of Belfast aforesaid; all for the Time being, shall be Trustees for executing the several Powers contained herein, and also in the said former Act, so far as the same is not altered hereby; and that from and after the First Day of May next, the Power and Authority as Trustees under the said former Act, of all Persons named therein, or since appointed, pursuant thereto, shall cease and determine, and shall be only vested in the said Trustees hereby appointed, and their Successors for the Time being, to be by them used and exercised in such particular Manner, and under such Restrictions and Limitations, as are herein particularly mentioned, and that the said Trustees be divided into three Committees, and the said Road into three Divisions; that the first of the said Committees

tees shall consist of the Governor and Custos Rotulorum of the County of Down; the Bishops of Down and Connor, and of Dromore; the Knights of the Shire for the said County of Down; and the Burgesses in Parliament of the said Borough of Hillsborough; the Lords of the said Manors of Gill-Hall, Dromore and Hillsborough; the Justices of the Peace for the said County of Down; the Dean of Dromore; the Archdeacon of Down, and his resident Curate at Hillsborough aforesaid; the Rector of Dromore, and his resident Curate; the Vicar of Seapatrick, and his resident Curate; the Seneschals of the said Manors of Gill-Hall, Dromore and Hillsborough, and the Sovereign of Hillsborough aforesaid, all for the Time being: That the second of such Committees shall consist of the Governor, and Custos Rotulorum of the said County of Down; the Bishop of Down and Connor; the the Knights of the Shire for the said County of Down; and Burgesses in Parliament for the said Boroughs of Lisburn and Belfast; the Lords of the said Manors of Kilultagh, Castlereagh and Slatueils, Drumbracklin, Holywood, and Belfast; the Justices of the Peace for the said County of Down; the Archdeacon of Down, and his resident Curates of Drumbo and Drumbeg aforesaid, respectively; the Rector of Lisburn aforesaid, and his resident Curate, the Rector of Knock and Bredagh

CHAP. XV.

Fff 2

CHAP. XV.

dagh aforesaid, and his resident Curate; the Vicar of Belfast aforesaid, and his resident Curate; the Seneschals of the said Manors of Kilultagh, Castlereagh, and Slatucils, Drumbracklin, Holywood and Belfast, and the Sovereign of Belfast aforesaid, all for the Time being; and that the Third of such Committees shall consist of the Governor and Custos Rotulorum of the said County of Antrim; the Bishop of Down and Connor; the Knights of the Shire for the said County of Antrim; the Burgesses in Parliament for the said Boroughs of Lisburn and Belfast; the Lords of the said Manors of Kilultagh and Belfast; the Justices of the Peace for the said County of Antrim; the Rector of Lisburn aforesaid, and his Resident Curate; the Vicar of Belfast aforesaid, and his Resident Curate; the Seneschals of the said Manors of Kilultagh and Belfast, and the Sovereign of Belfast aforesaid, all for the Time being; that so much of the said Road as reaches from Bann-Bridge aforesaid, unto the Northermost Boundary of the Lands of Maghry-garry, commonly called Blairis Moor, shall be, and be called the first Division thereof; that so much of the said Road as reaches from the End of the said first Division of Blairis Moor aforesaid, unto the Town of Belfast aforesaid, lying entirely within the said County of Down, and the Northermost Part of Which is commonly called the Upper Road, shall

shall be, and be called the second of such Divisions; and that such part of the said Road, as lies between the Towns of Lisburn and Belfast aforesaid, lying mostly in the said County of Antrim, and commonly called the Lower Road, shall be, and be called the third of such Divisions.

CHAP. XV.

And be it further Enacted by the Authority aforesaid, That the first of the said Divisions of the said Road, with the Tolls thereof, and all Matters relative thereto, shall, from the Time aforesaid, be committed to the Care and Government of the first of the said Committees; the second of the said Divisions, in like Manner, to the second of the said Committees; and the third of the said Divisions, also in like Manner, to the third of the said Committees; and that each of the said Committees respectively, may appoint and remove a Clerk and Treasurer, Collectors, or Receivers of Tolls, and Surveyors, and all other Officers, in such Manner as the Trustees under the said former Act are impowered to appoint, and remove a Clerk, Treasurer, Collectors, or Receivers of Tolls, Surveyors, or other Officers; and that each of such Clerks, and other Officers, shall have such and the same Powers and Capacities, relative to such of the said Divisions, as he shall be so appointed for, as

Ggg the

CHAP. XV. the Clerk, or other such Officer of the said Trustees, acting under the said former Act, now hath, or would have, relative to the said Road, while entire, and not divided; but that no Clerk, or Treasurer, or other Officer, to be appointed by Virtue of this present Act, shall have or be allowed a greater Salary than Ten Pounds yearly; and that each of the said Committees shall have a Common Seal, and shall within, and relative to their said several and respective Divisions of the said Road, and all Matters relative thereto, respectively, be vested with all such Powers, Capacities, and Authorities, both with respect to the Things to be done, and the Number of Persons to join in doing such Things, and otherwise, in all Respects whatsoever, as the Trustees at present acting under the said former Act, by Virtue thereof, or of any other Law now in being, have, or should have, or are, or would be vested with, relative to the said Road, if this Act had not been made; and that all Persons, who by the said former Act, and if the same remained unaltered, would be bound to yield any Submission or Obedience, in any Matter or Matters relative to the said Road, unto the said Trustees under the said former Act, or any Number of them, shall, from and after the Time aforesaid, be bound to yield the like Submission and Obedience, in every

the

the like Matters, so far as relates to any
of the said Divisions of the said Road,
unto such of the said Committees, as by
this Act are appointed to have the Care and
Government of such Division of the said
Road, or in Default of yielding such Submission or Obedience, shall be subject to
such Penalties as are appointed by the said
former Act; for Recovery of which, such
Committees, respectively, may proceed, as,
according to the said former Act, the Trustees acting under the same might, in the
like Cases, have proceeded; but that none
of the said Committees shall have any
Power to intermeddle with any Part of any
other of the said Divisions of the said
Road, or any Part of the Tolls thereof, or
any other Matter relative thereto; neither
shall any Person, who shall have paid Toll
at any Gate or Turnpike on one of the
said Divisions, for any Carriage, Cattle, or
Beast, be therefore excused from paying
Toll on the same Day, for the same Carriage, Cattle, or Beast, if passing through
any Gate or Turnpike on any other of the
said Divisions.

CHAP.
XV.

And be it further Enacted by the Authority aforesaid, with regard to the Two
Days Statute Work, by the said former
Act appropriated to the Repair of the
said Road, that the said Two Days Work

CHAP.
XV.
of the Inhabitants of the Parish of Seapatrick aforesaid, and of so much of the Parish of Blairis, as lies within the Manors of Hillsborough and Kilworlin, or either of them, and of all other Parishes in the said County of Down, through which the said first Division of the said Road passes, shall, from and after the said first Day of May next, be applied to the Repair of the said first Division of the said Road; That the like Work of the Inhabitants of the Remainder of the said Parish of Blairis, and of the other Parishes through which the said second Division of the said Road passes, shall in like Manner be applied to the Repair of the said second Division of the said Road, and the like Work of the Inhabitants of such Parishes in the said County of Antrim, as the said third Division of the said Road passes through, shall in like Manner be applied to the Repair of the said third Division of the said Road; and that such Inhabitants, and the Surveyors of the High-Ways, in the said Parishes respectively, shall, from the Time aforesaid, be bound to obey the said Committees, or such as they shall appoint, with regard to making Returns of the Persons bound to perform such Work, and to the Time and Place of performing such Work as heretofore, by the said former Act, such Inhabitants

tants and Surveyors of the High-Ways, were bound to obey the Trustees acting under the said former Act, or the Surveyor or Surveyors by them appointed; and that such Committees, or any of the Surveyors, by them respectively appointed to direct the Application of the said Statute Work, may compound with any of the said Inhabitants for a Sum of Money, to be paid in lieu of his said Two Days Work, at any Rate not less than One Shilling for a Day's Work of a Man and Horse, not less than Six-pence for a Man: And that if any of such Inhabitants shall fail to pay such Composition-Money on Demand, or to perform his said Work, when legally warned, at the Time and Place for that Purpose appointed, that for every such Default, he shall not only be obliged to pay such his Composition-Money, or the Penalty for neglecting to perform his Work, according to the said former Act, as the Case may happen to be, but shall also forfeit the further Sum of Two Shillings and Six-pence, to be recovered and levied, as well as the said Composition-Money, and the said Penalty under the said former Act, in the same Manner as the said Penalty imposed by the said former Act, for neglecting to perform the said Work, is directed to be recovered and levied. All Which Sums so to be ledied, shall be paid to the Overseer of the said Road, and applied to the Repair of the same, as the said Committee shall direct, within such Division as the said Work such Inhabitants ought to have been applied to.

And be it further Enacted by the Authority aforesaid, That when and so often as a Surplus of the Money arising from the Tolls of any of the said three Divisions, amounting to the Sum of One Hundred Pounds, shall, after repairing the Roads of such Division, and discharging the Interest of all the principal Money then chargeable on the Tolls thereof, according to the true Intent and Meaning of this Act, remain in the Hands of the Treasurer or Receiver of such Division, then, and so often, the Committee of such Division are hereby required and impowered to apply the same by Ballot, to the Discharge of so much of the principal Money then chargeable on the Tolls of such Division, in like Manner, and after such Notice of such ballotting, as by the said former Act, the Trustees thereof are required and impowered to apply the Surplus Money in their Treasurer or Receivers Hands, when amounting to the Sum of Two Hundred Pounds; and whenever the Surplus Money so collected, and in the Hands of the

the Treasurer or Receiver of any one or two of the said Committees, shall exceed the Principal and Interest then remaining due, and chargeable on the Tolls of the Division or Divisions of the said Road, committed to the Care of such Committee or Committees respectively, or that all such Debts shall have been discharged, and any Money amounting to Fifty Pounds beyond the Sum requisite to keep such Division or Divisions of the said Road in Repair, shall remain in the Hands of the Treasurer or Receiver of any such Committees respectively, then, and so often, such Committee or Committees are hereby required to pay the same over to such other Committee or Committees, to enable them to discharge their Debts by Ballot as aforesaid; for which Payments, the Treasurer or Treasurers, Receiver or Receivers respectively, who shall receive the same, shall give Receipts to the Treasurer or Treasurers paying the same; and this Method shall be followed, until the whole Debts due and chargeable on the Tolls of each and every of the said Divisions of the said Road shall be discharged; but where only one of the said Committees shall leave such Surplus Money in their Treasurer or Receivers Hands, as aforesaid, then they are hereby required to divide the same equally, and pay one Half only

CHAP.
XV.

only to the Treasurer or Receiver of each of the said other Committees, unless one of the said Committees shall, before that Time, have discharged its whole Debt, in which Case the Whole of the said Surplus shall be paid to the Treasurer or Receiver of the other of the said Committees.

And Whereas by the former Act, fifteen or more Trustees are required to make a Quorum, in certain Cases; Be it Enacted by the Authority aforesaid, That in all such Cases, Five or more of the Trustees may be enabled to execute the Powers of this Act in this Division.

And be it further Enacted by the Authority aforesaid, That the Trustees of the said first Committee, or any Five or more of them, shall hold their first Meeting at Hillsborough, in the County of Down, on the second Monday in the Month of May next, in order to appoint Officers, and do other Acts requisite for taking upon them, and beginning the Execution of the Trusts hereby reposed in them; that the Trustees of the said second Committee shall hold their first Meeting for the like Purposes, at Breda, in the County of Down, on the third Monday in the same Month; and that the said third Committee shall hold their

their first Meeting for the like Purposes, CHAP.
at Lisburn, in the County of Antrim, on XV.
the third Monday in the same Month; that
the subsequent Meetings of each of the said
three Committees respectively, shall be held
by Adjournment, or otherwise, as, accord‐
ing to the Laws now in being, the Meet‐
ings of the Trustees under the said former
Act should have been holden; and that at
all such Meetings, each Trustee shall de‐
fray his own Charges and Expences: And
that no Trustee, appointed by this Act,
shall be capable of any Place of Profit a‐
rising out of, or by Reason of the Tolls
or Duty by this Act laid or granted.

And for the better discovering and pu‐
nishing all Persons who shall break, pull
down, or destroy, or attempt to break,
pull down, or destroy any Gate, Bar, or
Turn-pike, or Toll-house now being, or
which hereafter, pursuant to this Act, shall
be fixed or built on any Part of the said
Road; Be it Enacted by the Authority a‐
foresaid, That every Person so offending,
and being thereof convicted upon Indictment
before the Justices of Assize and Goal De‐
livery, or before the Justices of the Peace
at their General Quarter Sessions, shall,
for every such Offence, forfeit the Sum of
Twenty Pounds, and shall also suffer
Imprisonment in the common Goal of the

J i i County,

County, without Bail or Mainprize, for the Space of Six Months, and until such Fine shall be paid, the one Half of which shall be to the Use of His Majesty, His Heirs and Successors, and the other Half shall be applied to the Repair of such of the said Divisions of the said Road, as the said Offence shall be committed upon, and for that Purpose shall, by the Sheriff, or other Officer who levies the same, be paid to the Treasurer or Receiver of such Division; and if any Person guilty of such Offence, shall discover and prosecute to Conviction any Accomplice of his, guilty of the same Offence, the Person so discovering and prosecuting, shall be pardoned for his said Offence, and all former Offences committed by him against this Act.

And be it further Enacted by the Authority aforesaid, That this Act, and so much of the said former Act, as is not hereby repealed or altered, shall continue in Force for the Term of Forty-one Years, to be computed from the said First Day of May next.

Provided nevertheless, that if at any Time before the Expiration of the said Term of Forty-one Years, all Parts of the said Road shall be sufficiently amended and repaired, and so adjudged by the Majority

jority of the Trustees aforesaid, for the Time being, that then after such Adjudication thereof by them made, and Payment of the Whole of the said Principal Money, and Interest now due, and of all such other Money as shall hereafter, by Virtue of this or the said former Act, be borrowed, with Interest for the same, and the Costs and Charges thereof, the said Tolls and Duties shall cease and determine; any Thing herein contained to the Contrary notwithstanding.

CHAP.
XV.

And be it further Enacted by the Authority aforesaid, That if any Suit shall be commenced against any Person or Persons for any Thing done in Pursuance of this Act, that in every such Case the Action shall be laid in the said Counties of Down, or Antrim, and not elsewhere, and the Defendant or Defendants, in such Action or Actions to be brought, may plead the General Issue, and give this Act, and the special Matter in Evidence at any Tryal to be had thereupon, and that the same was done in Pursuance, and by the Authority of this Act; and if it shall appear so to be done, or such Action or Actions shall be brought in any other County, that then the Jury shall find for the Defendant or Defendants, and upon such Verdict, or if the Plaintiff shall be nonsuited,

Chap. XV.
or discontinue his Action after the Defendant or Defendants shall have appeared, or if on any Demurrer Judgment shall be given against the Plaintiff, the Defendant or Defendants shall and may recover treble Costs, and have the like Remedy for the same, as any Defendant or Defendants hath or have in any other Cases by Law.

And be it Enacted by the Authority aforesaid, That the second Committee to whom the Tolls and Profits of the Gate, commonly called Jones Gate, are hereby granted, do and shall, from Time to Time, and at all Times hereafter account with, and pay to the third Committee, one full Moiety of all the Toll Revenue, Profits or Sums of Money which shall arise from, or be collected or received at or by the Keeper or Keepers of the said Gate, the same to be paid by four equal quarterly Payments in every Year, (that is to say) on every First Day of May, First Day of August, First Day of November, and First Day of February in every Year, the first Payment thereof to be made on the First Day of August next ensuing.

And be it further Enacted by the Authority aforesaid, That every Person purchasing one or more Ticket or Tickets at said

said Gate, for any Horse or Horses, Carriage or Carriages, or any Number of Cattle, by said Ticket or Tickets, shall and may, with such Horse and Horses, Carriage and Carriages, Beast or Beasts, pass on the Day he shall so purchase said Ticket or Tickets, Toll free, through all intermediate Gates, which are or shall be erected, into the Town of Belfast, either by the County of Antrim, or County of Down Road, and all Tickets purchased at any of the Gates near the Town of Belfast, either in the County of Down, or Antrim, shall likewise carry the Traveller through the said Gate, commonly called Jones Gate, without paying any further Toll at any of the said intermediate Gates.

And in order to apportion, in the most equal Manner, the several Debts or Sums of Money so borrowed and expended by the Trustees in said former Act mentioned, and to charge the same upon the three Committees aforesaid, according to the respective Value of the Income or Profit of each of the said Committees; Be it further Enacted by the Authority aforesaid, That the Marquis of Kildare, the Earls of Antrim, Donegal, Carrick, Hillsborough, Massareene, Clanbrassil, and Moyra; the Bishops of Down and Dromore; the Lord Annesly; the Knights of the Shire for the Counties of Down and Antrim,

CHAP. XV. Antrim, and the Members of Parliament representing the several Boroughs in the said Counties of Down and Antrim, or any five of them, be, and they are hereby constituted and made Trustees, and are fully impowered, authorized and required, to meet at Hillsborough, in the County of Down, on the First Monday after the Twenty-fourth Day of June next ensuing, at Ten of the Clock in the Morning, and to adjourn from Time to Time, and from Place to Place, as they shall find expedient, and with all convenient Speed to enquire into, and ascertain the several Sums of Money so borrowed as aforesaid, and which still remain due and unpaid, and the Interest due thereupon, and the Names of the several Persons respectively to whom such Sums are due, and also to enquire into, and ascertain, with as much Preciseness as may be, the annual Value, Income or Revenue of each of the said Gates, so allotted to the said three Committees respectively, and to allot and appoint to each of the said Committees such a Portion, Share, or Part of the said Debt, as shall bear the same Proportion to the Whole Debt, as the Tolls or Income of the Gates allotted to such Committee, bears to the Whole Revenue, or Income of all the Gates, which are or were erected on the said Turnpike Road; and to prevent any Apprehensions of Partiality in the allotting or appointment

ment of the Debts of the said Committee respectively; Be it Enacted by the Authority aforesaid, That the particular Debts of each Committee shall be allotted and ascertained by Ballot in Manner following, (that is to say) two Boxes shall be provided with Covers, and into one of them shall be put three Pieces of Paper of equal Size, on one of which shall be written, First Committee; on another shall be written, Second Committee; and on another shall be written, Third Committee; and into the other Box shall be put a Number of Pieces of Paper of equal Size, equal to the Number of Debentures then standing out and unpaid, each of which Pieces of Paper shall contain in writing the Number of one of the said Debentures, the Sum for which, and the Interest thereof then due, and the Name of the Person to whom the same was given, and all said Pieces of Paper shall be shaked together, and then a Person shall draw out of the first mentioned Box, one of the said three Papers, mentioning one of the said three Committees; and out of the second mentioned Box shall be drawn Pieces of Paper, containing Entries of Debentures, as equal as may be, by Principal and Interest, but not less than the whole Debt of the Committee, the Number of which shall have been drawn as aforesaid, and the Debentures, so drawn as aforesaid, shall stand, and

Chap. XV. and be the Debt of said Committee, and that the several Debts of the other two Committees be ascertained by Ballotting in like Manner.

Provided always, That if the last drawn Debenture of either of the two Committees which are drawn first out of the Box, shall exceed the Sum mentioned or ascertained as the Debt of such Committee, then, and in that Case, the said Trustees are hereby impowered, and required to set off, or assign the Surplus of such Debenture or Debentures, in such Manner, and to such Person or Persons, as the Creditors shall at the Time of Drawing, or immediately after, agree upon. And in case the said Creditors shall not immediately agree on, and propose such Manner of Assigning such Overplus, then the said Trustees are hereby authorized and required to set off, allot, and assign the same in such Manner, as to them shall seem most expedient, and to make the same the Debt of any of the Creditors of the last or undrawn Committee; and the said Trustees are hereby required to meet at the Time and Place aforesaid, to adjourn from Time to Time, and from Place to Place, as they shall judge expedient.

Provided

Provided allways, that the Execution of the said Trust shall be fully compleated on or before the Twenty-ninth Day of September, One thousand seven hundred and sixty-two, and all and every Act and Acts of the said Trustees, relative to the Matters herein before mentioned, which shall be done after the said Twenty-ninth Day of September, shall be, and are hereby declared to be absolutely null and void.

And be it further Enacted by the Authority aforesaid, That this Act shall be deemed, adjudged, and taken to be a Publick Act; and be judicially taken Notice of as such, by all Judges, Justices, and other Persons whatsoever, without specially pleading the same.

AN ACT

FOR

The Relief of

INSOLVENT DEBTORS.

DUBLIN:

Printed by BOULTER GRIERSON, Printer to the King's most Excellent Majesty. MDCCLXII.

(129)

AN

ACT

FOR

The Relief of

INSOLVENT DEBTORS.

CHAP. XVI.

WHEREAS several persons have been for a long Time, and are now, confined for Debt in several Goals in this Kingdom,

CHAP.
XVI.

And

CHAP. XVI.
And Whereas it is reasonable to make some Provision for the Relief of such of them as shall be willing to satisfy their Creditors to the utmost of their Power; for Which Purpose,

Be it Enacted by the King's Most Excellent Majesty, by and with the Advice and Consent of the Lords Spiritual and Temporal, and Commons in this Parliament assembled, and by the Authority of the same, That from and after the First Day of May, One thousand seven hundred and sixty-two, it shall and may be lawful, to and for all and every Person and Persons, Who were, on the Twenty-fifth Day of October, One thousand seven hundred and sixty, actual Prisoners in the Custody of any Goaler or Goalers, or Keeper of any Prison respectively, upon any Execution, Writ, Action, Attachment, Costs, Contempt, or any Process Whatsoever, for or by Reason of any Debt or Demand Whatsoever, Without Fraud or Collusion With their Creditors or others, and Who have ever since continued in Prison, to exhibit a Petition before the End of Trinity Term, One thousand seven hundred and sixty-six to any Court of Law from Whence the Process issued, upon Which such Prisoners Were or shall be respectively confined, or to the

CHAP.
XVI.

the Court into which any such Prisoners have been or shall be removed by Habeas Corpus, setting forth a just and true Account of all the Real and Personal Estate of which he, she or they, so petitioning, or any Person or Persons in Trust for him, her or them, is, are, or shall be intitled to, at the Time of his, her or their so petitioning, and of all Incumbrances and Charges, if any there be, affecting the same; and also a just and true Account of all the Real and Personal Estate which he, she or they, so petitioning, or any Person or Persons in Trust for him, her or them, or for his, her, or their Use, is interested in, or intitled unto, in Possession, Reversion, Remainder or Expectancy, to the best of the Belief of every such Prisoner or Prisoners, and so far as his, her or their respective Knowledge extends concerning the same; and likewise a just and true Account of all Securities wherein any Part of the Estates of any such Prisoner or Prisoners consists, of all the Deeds, Evidences, Writings, Books, Bonds, Notes and Papers concerning the same, or relating thereto, and in whose Hands the same respectively are, and the Names and Places of Abode of the Witnesses to all such Securities, Bonds and Notes, and where they are respectively to be met with, so far as his, her or their
Knowledge

Knowledge extends concerning the same: And before any such Petition shall be received by any such Court, every such Prisoner or Prisoners shall cause to be given or left unto, or for all and every the Creditor or Creditors at whose Suit any such Prisoner or Prisoners stand charged, or his, her or their Executors or Administrators, or at his, her or their usual Place of Abode, or to or for his, her or their Attorney or Agent last employed in any such Action or Actions, in Case any such Creditor or Creditors, his, her or their Executors or Administrators reside upwards of Ten Miles from the Goal where such Prisoner is confined, or cannot be then met with, fourteen Days at least before any such Petition shall be presented and received, a Notice in Writing, signed with the proper Name or Mark of every such Prisoner or Prisoners, importing therein, that such Prisoner or Prisoners doth, or do intend to petition the Court from whence the Process issued, upon which he, she or they stand charged, or from which the Habeas Corpus issued, upon which such Prisoner has been removed, or instead of serving such Notice as above said, it shall be sufficient to all Intents and Purposes that the same be inserted in three several Dublin Gazettes, containing the Name, Trade, or Occupation, and last Place of Abode of every

CHAP. XVI.

every such Prisoner, and of the Prison wherein he, or she, is confined, and of his or her Intention to take the Benefit of this Act, for which there shall be paid Sixpence for each Person, and no more, the last of which shall be Twenty Days before the preferring of such respective Petitions, and an Affidavit of the due Service of every such Notice at the Time of presenting thereof, or the Gazettes, in which such Notice shall be inserted, shall be openly read in the Court to which any such Petition shall be preferred; and if such Court shall thereupon be satisfied of the Regularity of any such Notice or Notices, such Petition shall be received, and such Court shall thereupon, by Order or Rule, cause the Prisoner or Prisoners, so petitioning, to be brought up to such Court, on some certain Day, in such Order specified: And if any Creditor or Creditors of any such Prisoner or Prisoners, at whose Suit such Prisoner or Prisoners stands charged, his, her or their Executors or Administrators, shall appear in Person, or by his, her or their Attorney; or if any such Creditor or Creditors, his, her or their Executors or Administrators, shall neglect to appear in Person, or by his, her or their Attorney, such Court shall, in a summary Way, examine upon Oath, if the said Court shall think the same proper, into the Matter

Chap. XVI.

ter of such Petition, and hear what can or shall be alledged, on either Side, for or against the Discharge of any such Prisoner or Prisoners who shall so petition, and upon such Examination, every such Court is hereby required to administer to the Prisoner or Prisoners respectively, who shall so petition, an Oath; or if the Person be of the People called Quakers, an Affirmation, to the Effect following, (that is to say)

I, *A. B.* do swear, in the Presence of Almighty God, (*if a Quaker*, I do affirm) that the Account by me set forth in my Petition, presented to this Honourable Court, doth contain a full and true Account of all the Real and Personal Estate, Debts, Credits and Effects whatsoever, which I, or any in Trust for me, am in any respect intitled to, in Possession, Reversion or Remainder, except the Wearing Apparel and Bedding of or for me and my Family, and the Tools and Instruments of my Trade, or Calling, not exceeding Ten Pounds in Value in the Whole; and also a true Account of all Deeds, Writings, Books, Papers, Securities, Bonds and Notes relating thereto, and where the same respectively now are, and in whose Hands, to the best of my Knowledge, Remembrance and Belief; and what Charges are now affecting the real Estate I am now seized of, or intitled to,

(*if*

(if any such Prisoner shall be then seized of any real Estate) and that I have not, at any Time, before or since my Imprisonment, directly or indirectly sold, lessened, assigned, mortgaged, pawned, or otherwise disposed of, or made over in Trust, for myself, or otherwise, any Part of my real and personal Estate, whereby to have or accept any Benefit, Advantage, or Profit to myself or my Family, or with any View, Design, or Intent to deceive, injure, or defraud any of my Creditors.

So help me God.

And in case any such Prisoner or Prisoners shall, in open Court, take the said Oath, such Court may then immediately order the real and personal Estate, contained in such Account, to be by a short Indorsement on the Back of such Petition, and to be signed by the Prisoner, assigned and conveyed to such Creditor or Creditors of the said Prisoner as such Court shall think proper, subject nevertheless to all prior Incumbrances affecting the same; and the Estate, Interest and Property of such real and personal Estate, which shall belong to any such Prisoner, shall, by such Assignment and Conveyance, be vested in the Person or Persons to whom such Assignment or Conveyance shall be made, according to the Estate and Interest such Prisoner or Prisoners had therein respectively, and the Creditor or Creditors, to whom

CHAP. XVI. Whom any such Assignment or Conveyance shall be made, shall and may take Possession of, and sue in his, her or their Name or Names, for the Recovery thereof, in like Manner as such Prisoner or Prisoners might have done, and no Release of any such Prisoner or Prisoners, or any Trustee for him, her or them, subsequent to such Assignment or Conveyance, shall be pleadable, or be allowed of in Bar of any Action or Suit which shall be commenced by any such Assignee or Assignees, for the Recovery of any Part of the real or personal Estate of such Prisoner or Prisoners; and upon every such Assignment and Conveyance being executed by any such Prisoner or Prisoners, he, she or they shall be discharged out of Custody by Rule or Order of such Court, and such Rule or Order being produced to, and a Copy thereof being left with any such Sheriff, Goaler or Keeper of any Prison as aforesaid, shall be a sufficient Warrant to him to discharge every such Prisoner or Prisoners; and every such Sheriff, Goaler or Keeper, is hereby required, on having such Order produced to him, and a Copy thereof left with him, to discharge and set at Liberty forthwith every such Prisoner or Prisoners, who shall be ordered as aforesaid to be discharged, without taking any Fee, or detaining him or them in respect of any Demand of any such Sheriff, Goaler or Keeper, for or in respect of Chamber Rent,

or

or Lodging, or otherwise, or for any Fees; and no Magistrate, Sheriff, Goaler or Keeper shall afterwards be liable to any Action of Escape, or other Suit or Information on that Account, or for what he shall do in pursuance hereof, and he may plead the General Issue, and give the special Matter in Evidence; and the Person or Persons to whom the Estate and Effects of any such Prisoner or Prisoners shall be assigned and conveyed, shall, with all convenient Speed, sell and dispose of the same, and shall divide the net Produce thereof amongst all the Creditors of every such Prisoner and Prisoners, (if more than one) to whom the Prisoner shall be fairly and justly indebted, in Proportion to each Creditor's respective Debts, the Marshal, Goaler or Keeper to be considered as a Creditor for his Fees, rateably and in Proportion to their respective Debts, and shall render the Overplus (if any there be) to such Prisoner or Prisoners, his Heirs and Assigns; but in case the Person or Persons, at whose Suit any such Prisoner or Prisoners stood charged, shall not be satisfied with the Truth of any such Prisoner's Oath, and shall either personally, or by Attorney, desire further Time to inform him, her or themselves of the Matters contained therein, such Court may, upon proper Cause shewn by Affidavit, remand any such Prisoner or Prisoners, and direct him, her or them, and such

CHAP. XVI. Creditor or Creditors, to appear, either in Person or by Attorney, on some other Day to be appointed by such Court, some Time, at farthest, within the Term next following the the Time of such Examination, but sooner if such Court shall so think fit; and all Objections which shall be made, as to the Insufficiency in Point of Form, against any Prisoner's Schedule of his Estate and Effects shall be only made the first Time any such Prisoner shall be brought up; and if, at such Second Day, the Creditor or Creditors shall make Default in appearing, or shall be unable to discover any Estate or Effects of the Prisoner's omitted in the Account set forth in such his, her, or their Petition, then, and in such Case, such Court shall, by Rule or Order thereof, immediately cause the said Prisoner or Prisoners to be discharged upon his, her, or their executing such Assignment and Conveyance as aforesaid; and if any Prisoner, who shall petition to be discharged as aforesaid, shall refuse to take the Oath or Affirmation, or, taking the same, shall afterwards be detected, before such Court, of Falsity therein, or shall refuse to execute such Assignment and Conveyance as aforesaid, he, she, or they shall be presently remanded and continue in Goal.

And

CHAP. XVI.

And be it Enacted by the Authority aforesaid, That from and after the First Day of May, One thousand seven hundred and sixty-two, any Prisoner confined in any County or other Goal, above the Space of Twenty Miles distant from the City of Dublin, may, at any Time before the First Day of May, One thousand seven hundred and sixty-six, prefer a Petition to the Court from whence any such Process issued, in like Form and Manner, as the Petitions herein before mentioned, and an Affidavit to the Purport, as Affidavits are herein before directed to be made, being made, or such Gazettes, as aforesaid, produced to such Court, and delivered into such Court with such Petition, such Court, on being satisfied of the Truth of such Affidavit, or on producing such Gazettes as aforesaid, may, and is required to make a Rule or Order, to cause the Prisoner or Prisoners, so petitioning, to be brought to the next Assizes which shall be holden for the County or Place where he, she, or they are imprisoned; and the Creditor or Creditors, his, her, or their Executors or Administrators, at whose Suit any such Prisoner or Prisoners is or shall be charged, shall, by Rule or Order of such Court, be ordered to appear at the said next Assizes, and such Judge or Judges of Assize respectively, shall appoint a Time for

CHAP. XVI. for hearing the Matter at such Assizes, upon every such Petition, and upon the Appearance of such Creditor or Creditors; or in Default of Appearance in Person, or by Attorney, then, on producing a Copy or Copies of the Order or Orders of the said Court or Courts, such Judge or Judges of Assize shall there, in a summary Way, examine into the Matter of every such Petition, and hear what can or shall be alledged on either Side, for or against the Discharge of such Prisoner or Prisoners; and upon every such Examination, such Judge and Judges of Assize, is and are hereby impowered and required, respectively, to administer or tender to every such Prisoner, the same Oath as herein before is directed, and to make such Order in the Premisses, as to him or them shall seem meet, and to proceed in the same Manner, concerning the Discharge of any such Prisoner or Prisoners, and to give the same Judgment, Relief, and Directions relating thereto, as any Court out of which any Process issued against any Prisoner or Prisoners, is herein before impowered and directed to do; and every such Order shall be as effectual and valid, as if the same had been made in the Court out of which the Process issued, upon which any such Prisoner was charged, and the same shall be made a Record of the Proceedings at such Assizes, and a Copy thereof

shall

shall be from thence transmitted to the Court from whence the Process, against such Prisoner or Prisoners discharged, issued, signed by the Judge or Judges of Assize, to be a Record of the said Court, and to be kept as such amongst the other Records thereof.

And be it Enacted by the Authority aforesaid, That from and after the First Day of May, One thousand seven hundred and sixty two, such of the said Prisoners, as are charged in Execution upon Decrees obtained before Judges of Assize upon Civil Bills, may, at any Time before the First Day of November, One thousand seven hundred and sixty two, prefer a Petition to the Judge or Judges of Assize which shall be holden for the County or Place where he, she, or they are imprisoned, in like Form and Manner as the Petitions herein before mentioned, provided such Prisoner or Prisoners shall cause to be given, or left to or for all and every the Creditor and Creditors at whose Suit he, she, or they stand charged in Execution as aforesaid, or his, her, or their Executors or Administrators; or in case any such Creditor or Creditors, or the Executors or Administrators of such Creditor or Creditors, cannot be met with, or his or their Attorney at Law, Agent last employed for him or them, or at his, her,

her, or their usual Place of Abode, twenty Days at least before the Assizes, a Notice in Writing, signed with the proper Name or Mark of every such Prisoner or Prisoners, importing that such Prisoner or Prisoners doth or do intend to petition the Court at the next Assizes, to be discharged, and requiring him, her, or them to appear at the next Assizes, and also a true Copy of the said Petition and Account; and such Judge and Judges of Assize, upon the Appearance of such Creditor or Creditors, either in Person or by Attorney, or in Default thereof, then, on Proof of his, her, or their being duly served with such Notice, and a Copy of such Petition and Account, as herein before is directed, shall, in a summary Way, examine upon Oath, if such Judge or Judges of Assize shall think necessary, into the Matter of every such Petition, and hear what can or shall be alledged on either Side, for or against the Discharge of such Prisoner or Prisoners; and, upon every such Examination, such Judge and Judges of Assize, is and are hereby impowered and required respectively to administer or tender to every such Prisoner, the same Oath as is herein before directed, and to make such Order in the Premisses, as to him or them shall seem meet, and to proceed in the same Manner, concerning the Discharge of any such Prisoner or Prisoners, and to give the same

same Judgment, Relief, and Directions, relating thereto, as any Court, out of which
any Process issued against any Prisoner or
Prisoners, is herein before impowered and
directed to do.

CHAP.
XVI.

And be it Enacted by the Authority
aforesaid, That from and after the Time
aforesaid, it shall and may be lawful to
and for the Recorder of the City of Dublin,
at any Time before the First Day of November, One thousand seven hundred and ... ty
two, to receive the Petitions of the said
Prisoners who are confined in the Marshalsea of the said City of Dublin, upon Decrees, or otherwise, and to examine into the
Matters of the same, and to administer
the same Oaths, and to proceed in the same
Manner, concerning the Discharge of such
Prisoners respectively, and to give the same
Judgment, Relief, and Directions relating
thereto, as any Court, out of which any
Process issued against any Prisoner or Prisoners, is herein before impowered and directed
to do.

And Whereas great Numbers of Work-
men, skilful in the several Trades and Manufactures in this Kingdom, and also many
able Seamen and Mariners, and several other
unfortunate Persons, finding themselves unable to satisfy the whole of the respective

Ppp 2

Debts,

CHAP. XVI. Debts, and dreading the Misery of a Goal, have chose to leave their Employments and native Country, and have gone into Foreign Countries.

And Whereas their Continuance abroad must be of great Prejudice to this Kingdom: In order therefore to induce and enable such Persons to return, Be it Enacted by the Authority aforesaid, That all and every Debtor and Debtors, who was or were actually beyond the Seas, in Foreign Parts, on the Twenty-fifth Day of October, One thousand seven hundred and sixty, and have continued abroad ever since on account of their Debts, who shall return and surrender himself or themselves, on or before the First Day of May, One thousand seven hundred and sixty-three, unto the Marshal of the Marshalsea of the Four-Courts in Dublin, who is hereby required and impowered to receive and detain such Debtor or Debtors, surrendering as aforesaid, in order to their Discharge, as hereafter mentioned, shall, from and immediately after such Surrender as aforesaid, be deemed a Prisoner or Prisoners, within, and to all Intents and Purposes, and be intitled to the Benefit of this Act, upon preferring Petitions to the Court of King's Bench and Common Pleas, in such Manner as is herein before directed, with respect to the Persons who were in

actual

actual Custody on the Twenty-fifth Day of October, One thousand seven hundred and sixty, and shall, upon due Proof of the said Premisses, by the Oath of such Debtor or Debtors, be discharged in the same Manner, as if he, she, or they had been in Prison on the said Twenty-fifth Day of October, One thousand seven hundred and sixty, and continued therein as aforesaid; subject nevertheless, to the same Restrictions and Provisions, and a Compliance with the like Terms, Conditions and Qualifications, hereby imposed upon the said Prisoners actually in Custody upon the said Twenty fifth Day of October, One thousand seven hundred and sixty, and also subject to the Terms and Provisions relating to the Estate and Effects of such Prisoners as aforesaid, the Oaths herein before appointed to be taken by Prisoners in Custody on the said Twenty-fifth Day of October, One thousand seven hundred and sixty, excepted; instead whereof, the Person or Persons so surrendering, shall take an Oath in open Court, to the Effect following, which the said Judges, impowered to put this Act into Execution, are hereby required and impowered to administer, in such Manner as the Oaths herein before mentioned are to be administred.

I *A. B.*

CHAP. XVI.

I *A. B.* upon my corporal Oath, in Presence of Almighty God, do solemnly swear, protest, and declare (if a *Quaker*, do affirm) that I was actually on the Twenty-fifth Day of *October*, One thousand seven hundred and sixty, beyond the Seas in Foreign Parts, to wit, at   and that the Schedule, now delivered, and by me subscribed, doth contain, to the best of my Knowledge, Remembrance, and Belief, a full, just, true, and perfect Account and Discovery of all the real Estate, Goods, Effects, and other personal Estate, in any wise belonging to me, and also of all such Debts as are owing to me, or to any Person or Persons in Trust for me, and of all the Securities and Contracts whereby any Money now is, will, or may hereafter become payable, or whereby or wherefrom any Benefit or Advantage may accrue to me, or to my Use, or to any other Person or Persons in Trust for me, and the Names and Places of Abode of the several Persons from whom such Debts are due and owing; and that neither I, or any Person or Persons in Trust for me, am, is, or are seized of any real Estate in Possession, Reversion, Remainder, or Expectancy, or of any personal Estate of any Kind whatsoever, other than what are in the said Schedule contained, except my Wearing Apparel, and Bedding for myself and Family, my Working-Tools, and necessary Implements for my Occupation and Calling, not exceeding in the Whole, the Value of Ten Pounds;

Pounds; and that I have not directly or indirectly sold, lessened, or otherwise conveyed, disposed of in Trust, or concealed all or any Part of my real Estate, or my Goods, Chattles, Stocks, Debts, Securities, Contracts, or other personal Estate whatsoever, whereby to secure the same, so as to receive or expect any Profit or Advantage therefrom to myself or Family, or with any View, Intent, or Design to defraud or deceive any Creditor or Creditors to whom I am indebted in any wise howsoever, or prevent their recovering or obtaining their respective Debts.
So help me God.

Provided always, and be it Enacted by the Authority aforesaid, That nothing in this Act contained, shall extend, or be construed to hinder or prevent any Mortgage or Mortgages upon the Estate of such Prisoner or Prisoners, or of Persons intitled to the Benefit of this Act, or any Part thereof, to take Place upon the Lands, Tenements, or Hereditaments comprised in such Mortgage or Mortgages respectively, nor to prevent any Statutes, Staple Statute, Merchant Recognizance, or Judgment, Custodiam or Elegit, acknowledged by, or obtained against any such Prisoner or Prisoners, to take Place upon the Lands, Tenements, or real Effects of such Prisoner or Prisoners, in like Manner as such Mortgagees and Creditors by such Recognizance,

Judgments,

CHAP.
XVI.

Judgments, Custodiams and Elegits would have been preferred to other Creditors, of the real or personal Estate of such Prisoner and Prisoners respectively, if this Act had not been made; any Thing herein before contained to the contrary thereof, in any wise notwithstanding.

Provided always, That the Discharge of any Person by Virtue hereof, shall not acquit any other Person from such Debt, Sum or Sums of Money, or any Part thereof, but that all others shall be answerable for the same, in such Manner as they were before the passing hereof.

And be it Enacted by the Authority aforesaid, That if any such Prisoner, or Fugitive, shall deliver in any false or untrue Account of his or her Estate or Effects, or shall designedly conceal, and not insert in the Account he or she shall deliver in, and subscribe as aforesaid, any Books, Papers, Securities or Writings, relating to his or her Estate and Effects, with Intent to defraud his or her Creditor or Creditors, and shall be thereof convicted on an Indictment, he or she so offending, shall be adjudged a Felon, and suffer as such, without Benefit of Clergy.

Provided

Provided allways, and be it Enacted by the Authority aforesaid, That if the Estate and Effects of any Prisoner or Prisoners, or Fugitive or Fugitives, which shall be so assigned and conveyed, shall not extend to satisfy the whole Debt due to the Creditors as aforesaid, of the Prisoner who shall be so discharged, and the Fees and Chamber Rent due to the Warden, Marshal, or Goaler, then such Warden, Marshal, or Goaler, shall only receive a proportionable Dividend from such Prisoners Estates, in respect of such Fees and Chamber Rent, pro Rata, with the other Creditors, as aforesaid, of such Prisoner or Prisoners, or Fugitive or Fugitives.

CHAP. XVI.

Provided allways, and be it Enacted by the Authority aforesaid, That no Person to be discharged hereby, shall, at any Time hereafter, be imprisoned by reason of any Judgment or Decree, or for any Debt, Damages, Attachments, Contempts, Costs, Sum or Sums of Money contracted, incurred, occasioned, owing, or growing due before the Time of the Discharge of such Persons in pursuance of this Act, but that upon every Arrest, Suit, Judgment, or Decree, or for such Debts, Damages, Attachments, Contempts, Costs, Sum and Sums of Money, it shall and may be lawful

CHAP. XVI.
ful for any Judge of the Court where the Process issued, upon shewing the Copy of the Order of such Prisoner's Discharge or Discharges, to release and discharge out of Custody such Prisoner or Prisoners as aforesaid, and every such Judge is hereby impowered and directed so to do.

Provided always, That in all Cases where mutual Credit shall have been given between such Prisoner or Prisoners, Fugitive or Fugitives, and any other Person or Persons, Bodies politick or corporate, before the Delivery of any Schedule or Inventory of the Estate and Effects of such Prisoner or Prisoners, Fugitive or Fugitives, then, and in every such Case, nothing more shall be deemed to be vested by any Assignment which shall be made, in pursuance thereof, as the Estate or Effects of such Prisoner or Prisoners, than what shall appear to be due to him, her or them respectively, upon the Ballance of Accounts when truly stated.

And be it Enacted by the Authority aforesaid, That it shall and may be Lawful to and for the said respective Courts, who shall discharge such Prisoner or Prisoners, Fugitive or Fugitives, in pursuance hereof, on the Petition of any Creditor of such Prisoner or Prisoners, Fugitive or Fugitives, to any such Court complaining of any Insufficiency,

sufficiency, Fraud, Mismanagement, or other Misbehaviour of any of the Creditors of such Prisoner or Prisoners, Fugitive or Fugitives, to whom the Estate and Effects of such Prisoner or Prisoners, Fugitive or Fugitives, shall have been assigned in pursuance hereof, to order the respective Parties concerned to attend such Court on the Matter of every such Petition at some certain Time, in such Order to be mentioned; and every such Court, on hearing the Parties concerned therein, is hereby authorized to make, order, and give such Directions in the Premisses, for the prudent, just and equitable Management or Distribution of the said Estate and Effects, for the Benefit of the respective Creditors, as aforesaid, of such Prisoner or Prisoners, Fugitive or Fugitives, as such Court shall think fit.

And be it Enacted by the Authority aforesaid, That such Persons as are confined upon Writs of Excommunicatio Capiendo, may, at any Time, from and after the First Day of May, One thousand seven hundred and sixty-two, prefer a Petition to the Lord High Chancellor, setting forth the Circumstances of his, her, or their Case, with an Affidavit, verifying the material Facts contained in the same; and that it shall and may be lawful to and for the said Lord Chancellor to discharge such Person or Persons, if he shall judge it proper so to do, upon such Terms as he shall think reasonable.

Provided allways, That nothing herein contained shall extend, or be construed to extend, to the Relief of any Prisoner with respect to any Debt which he or she shall stand charged with at the Suit of the Crown, or who was in Execution on the Twenty-fifth Day of October, One thousand seven hundred and sixty, at the Suit of any one Person, for any one Debt or Sum exceeding Two Hundred Pounds, or whose Debts amount in the Whole to One Thousand Pounds, or to any Fugitive who is indebted to any one Person in the Sum of Two Hundred Pounds, or whose Debts amount in the Whole to One Thousand Pounds; and such Prisoner or Prisoners, Fugitive or Fugitives, shall not be intitled to take any Benefit whatsoever under this Act.

And whereas it may happen that several Persons, who may claim or be intitled to the Benefit of this Act, are seized of an Estate Tail in any Freehold, Lands, Tenements or Hereditaments, which Intail, with the Remainders expectant thereon, they have, by Law, Power to defeat and bar, either by levying a Fine or Fines,

or

or suffering a Recovery or Recoveries, and thereby said Freehold, Lands, Tenements and Hereditaments, should be liable to the payment of their Debts, and be delivered up according to the Terms of this Act, for the Benefit of their Creditors.

CHAP. XVI.

Be it Enacted by the Authority aforesaid, That in every such Case, such Person or Persons, so seized as aforesaid, and who shall be intitled unto, and claim the Benefit of this Act, shall, to all Intents and Purposes whatsoever, be deemed and taken to be seized of such Lands, Tenements, and Hereditaments in Fee simple, and the same shall be delivered up to the Creditor or Creditors, in the same Manner as if such Person or Persons had actually levied a Fine or Fines, or suffered a common Recovery or Recoveries, and thereby had become seized in Fee-simple; any Law, or Construction of Law, to the Contrary in any Wise notwithstanding.

Provided always, That nothing herein contained shall extend, or be deemed, construed, or taken to extend, to give any Benefit, Ease, Discharge or Relief to any Person or Persons whatsoever, from any Debt for Rent, or Arrears of Rent, which became due and payable out of any Lands, Tenements, or Hereditaments, where he,

CHAP. XVI.
she or they owing such Rent, or Arrears of Rent, or any other Person or Persons deriving by, from, or under him, her, or them, is, or are, in the Possession of all or any such Lands, Tenements, or Hereditaments, out of which such Rent was payable.

Provided further, That when any Rent, not exceeding Two Years Rent, shall be due to any Person or Persons from such Prisoner or Prisoners at the Time of his, her or their respective Discharges, in respect to any Messuages, Lands, or Tenements, no Goods or Chattles then being in or upon the respective Premisses liable to be distrained, shall be assigned in Manner aforesaid, but shall be transferred to such Landlord or Landlords, or some Person in Trust for him or them respectively, towards Satisfaction of the Rent then due, not exceeding Two Years Rent as aforesaid, unless the Creditor or Creditors, to whom such Assignment shall be made, shall, by Writing under his or their Hand or Hands respectively, before such Assignment shall be made, agree to pay or satisfy to such Landlord or Landlords, the Rent to him or them respectively due, not exceeding Two Years Rent as aforesaid.

Provided

CHAP. XVI.

Provided also, That no Person who, as Guardian, Trustee, Executor or Administrator, is indebted to any Person or Persons, shall be intitled to any Benefit or Relief from this Act.

Provided also, That all Persons, who have conveyed, imbezzled, or converted to their own Use any Monies, Goods, Wares or Merchandizes, of Persons who have employed and intrusted them, shall be excluded from receiving any Benefit or Advantage by this Act.

And whereas the several Persons, whose Names are mentioned in the following Schedule, have been, by Misfortunes, rendered unable to satisfy the Whole of their respective Debts, and it is reasonable to make Provision for the Relief of such of them, as shall do their utmost for the Satisfaction of their Creditors, although none of the said Persons were Prisoners in actual Custody on the said Twenty-fifth Day of October, One thousand seven hundred and sixty, nor were beyond the Seas in foreign Parts on the said Twenty-fifth Day of October;

Be it Enacted by the Authority aforesaid, That it shall and may be lawful,

Sss 2   to

CHAP. XVI.

to and for all and every the Persons, whose Names are mentioned in the said Schedule, at any Time before the First Day of May, One thousand seven hundred and sixty-three, to exhibit a Petition or Petitions to his Majesty's Court of King's-Bench, or Court of Common-Pleas, in Dublin, setting forth the several Matters hereby directed to be set forth in the Petitions of Persons who were Prisoners in actual Custody on the Twenty-fifth Day of October, One thousand seven hundred and sixty, and the Court, to which such Petitions shall be respectively preferred, shall receive the same, and administer to the Person or Persons respectively, who shall petition, an Oath, or, if the Person be of the People called Quakers, an Affirmation, to the like Effect, as the Oath or Affirmation herein before directed to be taken by Fugitives, except that Part which mentions their being beyond Sea on the Twenty-fifth Day of October, One thousand seven hundred and sixty, which the Judges of either of the said Courts are hereby impowered and required to administer; and the said Court may, thereupon, make such Order for the Assignment and Conveyance of the Real and Personal Estate of such of the Persons, whose Names are mentioned in the said Schedule, as shall so petition, as is hereby directed with respect to the Real and Personal Estates

tates of Prisoners in actual Custody on the Twenty-fifth Day of October, One thousand seven hundred and sixty, and, upon every such Assignment and Conveyance being executed by the Person or Persons who shall so petition, the said Court shall make a Rule or Rules for the Discharge of the Person or Persons so petitioning, as if such Person or Persons was or were, at the Time of making said Rule or Rules, in the actual Custody of the Marshal of the Four-Courts of the City of Dublin; and the respective Estates and Effects of the said Persons shall be subject to the Terms and Provisions hereby imposed on the Estates and Effects of Prisoners in actual Custody upon the Twenty-fifth Day of October, One thousand seven hundred and sixty; and the said Persons shall be intitled to the like Benefit and Relief, and subject to the like Punishment, in Case of delivering a false and untrue Account of their Estates and Effects, or concealing the same, as is hereby directed with respect to Prisoners in actual Custody on the said Twenth-fifth Day of October, One thousand seven hundred and sixty.

And Whereas, Robert Tighe, late of the City of Dublin, Merchant, now a Prisoner confined for Debt in the Marshalsea of

CHAP. XVI.

the Four-Courts, having had very considerable Dealings in this Kingdom, and having sustained many Losses in Trade, failed in his Credit, and in the Month of May, One thousand seven hundred and fifty-five, withdrew himself from his Creditors, and soon after laid before them a fair Account of his Estate and Effects, and offered to deliver up his said Estate and Effects to his said Creditors, in Satisfaction and Discharge of their several Demands, to be rateably divided between them, to which Proposal several of them agreed, and others refused to accept of less than their full Demands, and the said Robert was, by Means thereof, obliged to abscond until the Month of January, One thousand seven hundred and fifty-eight, when the said Robert was arrested at the Suit of one of his said Creditors, and committed to the Prison of the then Sheriffs of the City of Dublin; and several Writs having been issued against the said Robert, he, the said Robert, was, in the Month of March, One thousand seven hundred and fifty-eight, committed a Prisoner to the Marshalsea of the Four-Courts, where the said Robert hath ever since continued: And in as much as the said Robert is willing to deliver up all his Effects to and for the Use of the said Creditors;

Be

Be it Enacted by the Authority afore-CHAP.
said, That upon his, the said Robert's XVI.
performing the Requisites required by this
Act, that he, the said Robert Tighe, shall
have the Benefit and Advantage thereof,
and be discharged from his said Imprisonment, notwithstanding the Debts owing
by the said Robert Tighe, exceed the Sum
limited by, and mentioned in, this Act.

Whereas James Hamilton, late of Carlow,
Esquire, but now of the Isle of Man, some
Time in the Year One thousand seven
hundred and thirty-six, failed in his Credit,
indebted to several Persons in considerable
Sums, and, at the Time of his Fail-
ure, the said James Hamilton was possessed
of several considerable Estates in Fee-
simple, which have ever since been in the
Possession of some of his Creditors; that
there then were, and still are, several Suits
depending relative to the Lordship and
Manor of Carlow, and several Accounts
relative to the said James Hamilton's Property, not yet settled; that the said James
Hamilton has retired to the Isle of Man, being apprehensive that his Person might be
arrested, and his Creditors want the Assistance of the said James Hamilton for the
settling said Suits and Accounts, who is

Ttt 2 now

CHAP.
XVI.

now in the Seventy-seventh Year of his Age; Be it therefore Enacted by the Authority aforesaid, That from and after the Twenty-fifth Day of December, in the Year of Our Lord One thousand seven hundred and sixty one, the Person of the said James Hamilton shall be freed and exempted from all Manner of Arrests, at the Suit of any Creditor or Creditors, for any Sum or Sums of Money which are now due, and owing by the said James Hamilton.

And Whereas Thomas Houghton, late of New-Ross, in the County of Wexford, Timber Merchant, did, in the Year One thousand seven hundred and fifty-two, fail in his Credit, and became a Bankrupt, and unable to satisfy his several Creditors; and many of them refusing to accept a Composition, he was obliged, shortly after, to withdraw himself out of this Kingdom, and live in Foreign Parts; Be it Enacted by the Authority aforesaid, That the said Thomas Houghton surrendering himself to the Marshal of the Marshalsea of the Four-Courts in Dublin, at any Time before the End of Trinity Term, which will be in the Year of Our Lord One thousand seven hundred and sixty six, shall be deemed within the Meaning, and be intitled to the Benefit of this Act, and may prefer a Petition to any Judge or Judges of any of the Courts at Law,

Law, held in the Four-Courts of Dublin, who are hereby required and impowered, respectively, to examine into the Matters of the same, and to discharge the said Thomas Houghton, by performing the Requisites herein before directed.

And Whereas several Suits at Law, and in Equity, have been heretofore commenced and carried on against George Reynolds, of Letterfyan, in the County of Leitrim, Esquire, for Recovery of the Estate of the said George Reynolds, or of a great Part thereof, which drove the said George to the Necessity of contracting Debts, and borrowing several considerable Sums of Money from different Persons, to enable the said George to defray the Expence of the said Suits, and defend his Title to his said Estate, and by a long continued Litigation of such Suits, and the great Expence occasioned thereby, the said George hath not been able to pay his said Debts, or to pay or keep down the growing Interest thereof.

And Whereas many of the Creditors of the said George, so long ago as the Year One thousand seven hundred and forty five, obtained Custodiams against the Whole of the Estate of the said George, and although one or more of them have been, from Time to Time, ever since in Possession and Receipt

CHAP. XVI.

of the Rents of the said Estate, yet, from the many contested Motions, which have been in the Court of Exchequer for several Years past, among the several Creditors of the said George Reynolds, who had Custodiams of the said Estate, at great Expence and Costs, all which, as usual in such Cases, have fallen upon the Lands, and, of course, upon the said George Reynolds, the Income of his said Estate hath been thereby almost exhausted therein.

And whereas, notwithstanding the said Reynolds's Estate hath been so in the Hands of some of his Creditors, yet many others of them, from Time to Time, issued Executions and other Writs against his Person: Wherefore, and to avoid the Miseries of a common Goal, the said George, for many Years past, hath been obliged to confine himself to his House, by reason of which he hath contracted many Disorders, and his Health and Constitution are greatly impaired, insomuch that he cannot live any Time, if not released from such his Confinement, and his Death might prove fatal to his Creditors.

And whereas the said George Reynolds is inclined and desirous, to the utmost of his Power, to satisfy his Creditors, and in Order thereto, to vest his Estate in Trustees

for

for Payment of his Debts, reserving thereout such Sum or Sums as the said Creditors, or the Majority of them, shall judge sufficient for his Support and Maintenance: And the said George, by repeated Advertisements in the Publick Papers, hath requested Meetings of his Creditors, in order to consult and agree upon Measures to be taken for carrying such the said Reynolds's Intention into Execution.

And Whereas at a Meeting of a considerable Number of said Creditors, and the Agents of others of them, Who could not attend in Person on the Fourteenth Day of January last, it was unanimously agreed, that it would be for the Benefit of said Creditors, to have the Estate so vested in Trustees, for the Payment of said Reynolds's Debts, and that Theophilus Jones, and Gorges Edmond Howard, both of the City of Dublin, Esquires, would be proper and fit Persons to execute such Trust, in case they would undertake it, and they having since consented thereto, and the Assistance and personal Attendance of the said George Reynolds upon such Trustees and his Creditors, being judged absolutely necessary, for carrying his said Intentions into Execution; Therefore, at the humble Petition of George Meares, Toby Peyton, Gorges Edmond Howard, Thomas Smyth, Patrick Dease, John Irwin, Philip Crampton,

CHAP. XVI.

ton, Michael Callagher, Susanna Plunket, Nicholas Darcy, John Taylor, John Tandy, and Robert Archbold, Creditors of the said George Reynolds, on Behalf of themselves and the rest of the Creditors of the said George Reynolds; Be it Enacted by the Authority aforesaid, That from the Time the Estate of the said George Reynolds shall be so vested in the said Persons as Trustees as aforesaid, and for the Purposes aforesaid, the Person of the said George Reynolds shall, from thenceforth, be freed, acquitted, and discharged of and from all Arrests, at the Suit of any Creditor or Creditors of the said George Reynolds, for any Sum or Sums of Money which is or are now due and owing by him; and that if the said George Reynolds shall be arrested, for or on Account of any such Debt or Debts, the said George Reynolds shall, from such Arrest or Arrests, be forthwith freed, released, and discharged.

Provided allways, That nothing contained in this Act, shall in any wise extend to the Benefit or Relief of Anne Goff, otherwise Bell, now a Prisoner at large in the Marshalsea of the Four-Courts, Dublin.

And Whereas by an Act of Parliament made in the Twenty-ninth Year of the Reign of his late Majesty King George the Second, Intituled, An Act for the Relief of the Creditors

Creditors of the Bank lately kept by *John Wil-* cocks and *John Dawson,* and of the Creditors of the Bank lately kept by *Joseph Fade* and *John Wilcocks,* and of the Creditors of the Bank lately kept by *Joseph Fade, Issachar Wilcocks* and *John Wilcocks,* and of the Creditors of the Bank lately kept by *Joseph Fade:* and for raising out of the Estates, Real and Personal, of *Richard Brewer,* late the Cash-keeper of the said *John Wilcocks* and *John Dawson,* the Sum due by the said *Richard Brewer* to the said *John Wilcocks* and *John Dawson;* 𝕿𝖍𝖊 𝕰𝖘𝖙𝖆𝖙𝖊, 𝕽𝖊𝖆𝖑 𝖆𝖓𝖉 𝕻𝖊𝖗𝖘𝖔𝖓𝖆𝖑, 𝖔𝖋 𝖙𝖍𝖊 𝖘𝖆𝖎𝖉 Richard Brewer, 𝖆𝖗𝖊 𝖛𝖊𝖘𝖙𝖊𝖉 𝖎𝖓 𝖙𝖍𝖊 𝕬𝖘𝖘𝖎𝖌𝖓𝖊𝖊𝖘 𝖎𝖓 𝖙𝖍𝖊 𝖘𝖆𝖎𝖉 𝕬𝖈𝖙 𝖓𝖆𝖒𝖊𝖉, 𝖋𝖔𝖗 𝖙𝖍𝖊 𝕻𝖚𝖗𝖕𝖔𝖘𝖊𝖘 𝖎𝖓 𝖙𝖍𝖊 𝖘𝖆𝖎𝖉 𝕬𝖈𝖙 𝖒𝖊𝖓𝖙𝖎𝖔𝖓𝖊𝖉.

𝕬𝖓𝖉 𝖜𝖍𝖊𝖗𝖊𝖆𝖘 𝖇𝖞 𝖙𝖍𝖊 𝖘𝖆𝖎𝖉 𝕬𝖈𝖙, 𝖎𝖙 𝖎𝖘 (𝖆𝖒𝖔𝖓𝖌 𝖔𝖙𝖍𝖊𝖗 𝕿𝖍𝖎𝖓𝖌𝖘) 𝕰𝖓𝖆𝖈𝖙𝖊𝖉, 𝖎𝖋 𝖙𝖍𝖊 𝖘𝖆𝖎𝖉 Richard Brewer 𝖘𝖍𝖔𝖚𝖑𝖉 𝖗𝖊𝖋𝖚𝖘𝖊 𝖙𝖔 𝖌𝖎𝖛𝖊 𝖎𝖓 𝖘𝖚𝖈𝖍 𝖕𝖆𝖗𝖙𝖎𝖈𝖚𝖑𝖆𝖗 𝕬𝖈𝖈𝖔𝖚𝖓𝖙, 𝖆𝖘 𝖎𝖓 𝖙𝖍𝖊 𝖘𝖆𝖎𝖉 𝕬𝖈𝖙 𝖒𝖊𝖓𝖙𝖎𝖔𝖓𝖊𝖉, 𝖔𝖗 𝖘𝖍𝖔𝖚𝖑𝖉 𝖇𝖊 𝖌𝖚𝖎𝖑𝖙𝖞 𝖔𝖋 𝖆𝖓𝖞 𝖜𝖎𝖑𝖋𝖚𝖑 𝕮𝖔𝖓𝖈𝖊𝖆𝖑𝖒𝖊𝖓𝖙 𝖔𝖗 𝕺𝖒𝖎𝖘𝖘𝖎𝖔𝖓 𝖙𝖍𝖊𝖗𝖊𝖎𝖓, 𝖔𝖗 𝖚𝖕𝖔𝖓 𝕰𝖝𝖆𝖒𝖎𝖓𝖆𝖙𝖎𝖔𝖓 𝖘𝖍𝖔𝖚𝖑𝖉 𝖇𝖊 𝖜𝖎𝖑𝖋𝖚𝖑𝖑𝖞 𝖋𝖔𝖗𝖘𝖜𝖔𝖗𝖓, 𝖘𝖍𝖔𝖚𝖑𝖉 𝖇𝖊 𝖆𝖉𝖏𝖚𝖉𝖌𝖊𝖉 𝖌𝖚𝖎𝖑𝖙𝖞 𝖔𝖋 𝕱𝖊𝖑𝖔𝖓𝖞, 𝖜𝖎𝖙𝖍𝖔𝖚𝖙 𝕭𝖊𝖓𝖊𝖋𝖎𝖙 𝖔𝖋 𝕮𝖑𝖊𝖗𝖌𝖞.

𝕬𝖓𝖉 𝖜𝖍𝖊𝖗𝖊𝖆𝖘 𝖇𝖞 𝖙𝖍𝖊 𝖘𝖆𝖎𝖉 𝕬𝖈𝖙 𝖎𝖙 𝖎𝖘 (𝖆𝖒𝖔𝖓𝖌 𝖔𝖙𝖍𝖊𝖗 𝕿𝖍𝖎𝖓𝖌𝖘) 𝖋𝖆𝖗𝖙𝖍𝖊𝖗 𝕰𝖓𝖆𝖈𝖙𝖊𝖉, 𝕿𝖍𝖆𝖙 𝖆𝖑𝖑 𝖆𝖓𝖉 𝖊𝖛𝖊𝖗𝖞 𝖔𝖙𝖍𝖊𝖗 𝕻𝖊𝖗𝖘𝖔𝖓 𝖔𝖗 𝕻𝖊𝖗𝖘𝖔𝖓𝖘, 𝖜𝖍𝖔 𝖙𝖍𝖊𝖓 𝖆𝖑𝖗𝖊𝖆𝖉𝖞 𝖍𝖆𝖉 𝖆𝖈𝖈𝖊𝖕𝖙𝖊𝖉 𝖔𝖋 𝖆𝖓𝖞 𝕿𝖗𝖚𝖘𝖙 𝖔𝖗 𝕿𝖗𝖚𝖘𝖙𝖘, 𝖆𝖓𝖉 𝖘𝖍𝖔𝖚𝖑𝖉 𝖜𝖎𝖑𝖋𝖚𝖑𝖑𝖞 𝖈𝖔𝖓𝖈𝖊𝖆𝖑 𝖆𝖓𝖞 𝖔𝖋 𝖙𝖍𝖊 𝕰𝖘𝖙𝖆𝖙𝖊, 𝕽𝖊𝖆𝖑 𝖔𝖗 𝕻𝖊𝖗𝖘𝖔𝖓𝖆𝖑, 𝖜𝖍𝖎𝖈𝖍 𝖇𝖊- longed

CHAP. XVI.
longed to the said Richard Brewer, thereby vested in the Assignees, and should not, on or before the First Day of March, One thousand seven hundred and fifty-seven, truly discover and disclose such Trusts and Estates in Writing to the Commissioners in the said Act named, or any Three or more of them, should be liable, and thereby stand chargeable with Double the Value of the Estate or Effects so to be concealed, to be recovered in such Manner, as in the said Act is directed.

And Whereas the said Richard Brewer is now in Custody of the Marshal of the Marshalsea of the Four-Courts, Dublin, on Account of the Demands of the said John Wilcocks and John Dawson.

And Whereas the Time limited by the said Act, for the said Richard Brewer's, and all other Persons, making a full and true Discovery of the Estate and Effects of the said Richard Brewer, is elapsed.

And Whereas the enlarging the Time for the said Richard Brewer's, and all other Persons making such Discovery, may be of Advantage to the said Wilcocks and Dawson, and to the said Richard Brewer respectively; Be it Enacted by the Authority aforesaid, That the said Richard Brewer, and

all

Georgii Tertii Regis.

CHAP.
XVI.

all and every Person or Persons, who already has, or have accepted of any Trust or Trusts, or hitherto concealed any of the Estate, Real or Personal, of the said Richard Brewer, shall be freed from, and shall not be subject or liable to, the Pains and Penalties in the said recited Act of the Twenty-ninth of His late Majesty, mentioned, or any of them, for, or on Account of secreting the Effects of the said Richard Brewer, or of the Bank lately kept by the said John Wilcocks and John Dawson, or for not discovering and disclosing such Trusts and Estates in Writing, to the said Commissioners, in the said Act named, or any Three or more of them, as by the said Act is directed; and in order that the said Richard Brewer, and every other Person or Persons, may make a Discovery of the Estate and Effects of the said Richard Brewer, or of any other Person or Persons, which by the said Act are made liable to the Debts of the said Bank.

And be it further Enacted by the Authority aforesaid, That the said Richard Brewer, and all and every Person or Persons, who shall at any Time before the First Day of January, in the Year One thousand seven hundred and sixty-four, make a Discovery of any Part of the Estate, Real or Personal, of the said Richard Brewer, or of any other Person or Persons, or which by the said

CHAP. XVI.

said Act are made liable to the Debts of the said Bank, not already come to the Knowledge of the said Commissioners in the said Act named, or any Three of them, or of the said Assignees, or Two of them, shall be allowed Five Shillings in the Pound, as a Reward, out of all such Estates and Effects, as by the Means of the said Richard Brewer, or such other Person or Persons, shall be recovered.

And be it further Enacted by the Authority aforesaid, That the said Richard Brewer may have Access to all the Books and Papers relative to the said Bank, upon his giving four Days previous Notice to the said Commissioners, and informing the said Commissioners, or any Three or more of them, of the Use or Uses for which he wants the Inspection of the said Books and Papers.

Provided always, and be it further Enacted by the Authority aforesaid, That if any of the Effects of the said Richard Brewer, secreted or concealed by himself, or any other Person or Persons in Trust for him, or on his Account, shall be discovered by any other Ways or Means, than by the Confession or Discovery of the said Richard Brewer, that he, the said Richard Brewer, shall, notwithstanding

standing any Thing in this Act contained to the contrary, be subject and liable to the Pains and Penalties mentioned in the said recited Act of the Twenty-ninth Year of His late Majesty.

And Whereas Thomas Hutchinson, late of the City of Dublin, Merchant, by unavoidable Losses in Trade, several Years ago became a Bankrupt, and not being able to satisfy his Creditors, was obliged to abscond, to avoid the Miseries of a Goal.

And Whereas some of his Friends have promised to collect among themselves a Sum of One Hundred Pounds, to be distributed amongst his Creditors, in Proportion to their several Demands; Be it Enacted by the Authority aforesaid, That the said Thomas Hutchinson, upon Payment of One Hundred Pounds into the Hands of John Barclay, of the City of Dublin, Merchant, on or before the First Day of May, One thousand seven hundred and sixty-two, shall for ever thereafter be freed and discharged from all further Demands of his present Creditors, or any of them, and from any Suit, Arrest, Action, or other Disturbance, on account of the Debts now owing by him: And the said John Barclay, his Executors or Administrators, shall distribute the said Sum of One Hundred Pounds

CHAP. XVI.
Pounds amongst all the Creditors of the said Thomas Hutchinson, who shall claim their respective Debts from the said John Barclay before the First Day of December, One thousand seven hundred and sixty-two, rateably, and in Proportion to their respective Debts.

Provided always, That nothing herein contained shall extend, or be construed to extend to bar, hinder, prevent, or delay Robert Lowry, of Milbery, in the County of Tyrone, Esquire, his Executors or Administrators, from having all such Remedy by Action, Suit, Arrest, or Execution, against Patrick M'Chryſtal and William M'Chryſtal, or either of them, for, or on Account of any Rent, or Arrears of Rent due by them, or either of them, to the said Robert Lowry, or to discharge the said William M'Chryſtal from any Imprisonment that he is, or may be under, at the Suit of the said Robert Lowry.

Provided always, That nothing herein contained shall extend, or be construed to extend to the Discharge of James Linihan or William Fitz-Gerald, now in Execution in the Goal of the County of Cork, at the Suit of Joseph Dean, Esquire.

Provided

CHAP. XVI. Provided allways, and be it Enacted by the Authority aforesaid, That no Person shall have the Benefit of this Act, who has been discharged by any former Act, for the Relief of Insolvent Debtors, unless his Name shall have been inserted in the Body of this Act, or in the Schedule thereto annexed.

The **Schedule** referred to by the annexed Bill.

Richard Pallisier, **Esquire, of the City of** Dublin; Martin Nowlan, **of the City of** Dublin, **Coach-maker;** Gregory French, late of **the City of** Dublin, **Merchant;** David Bomford, **of the City of** Dublin, **Grocer;** Patrick Dalton, **of the Town of** Longford, **Inn-keeper;** John Crowly, **of the City of** Cork, **Gentleman;** Thomas Faulkner, **of the City of** Dublin, **Merchant;** John Campion, **in the** Queen's-County, **Dealer;** Bryan Bannon, **of the City of** Dublin, **Flax Dresser;** William Hanna, **of the City of** Dublin, **Upholder;** Thomas Russel, **of the City of** Dublin, **Wool Comber;** James Fitz-Gerald, **of the City of** Dublin, **Vintner;** Charles Hyde Norcott, **of the County of** Cork, **Gentleman;** Robert Clibborn, **the younger,**

Younger, of the City of Dublin, Merchant; Michael Hanly, late of Silver-Mines, Inn-holder; Anne Evans, of Waterford, Widow, and her Daughter, Jane Evans; John Van Nost, of the City of Dublin, Statuary; Thomas White, of the City of Cork, Merchant; James Neal, of the City of Dublin, Glover; Perrott Davenport, of the City of Dublin, Gentleman; John Grace, of the City of Dublin, Sales-master; John Singleton, of the City of Dublin, Carpenter; William Ash, of Drogheda; John English, in the County of Meath, Linen-Weaver; Robert Power, of the City of Dublin, Merchant; John Roche, of the City of Limerick, Merchant; Richard Neeks, of Waterford, Merchant; Richard Shaw, of the City of Dublin, Esquire; Thomas Rahelly, of the City of Limerick; Mary Cape, of the City of Dublin, Widow; Michael Laughlin, of Kilkenny, Victualler; Edward Coppinger, of Cork, Merchant; James Connor, of Dublin, Linen Factor; John Sheridan, of Dublin, Vintner; Bryan O'Heale, of the County of Antrim, Gentleman; James Farrel, of Dublin, Cork-cutter; James Cunningham, of the City of Dublin, Merchant; John Molloy, of the City of Dublin, Merchant; William M'Cormack, of Dublin, Anchor-Smith; Richard Casey, of Cork, Cooper;

Cooper; William Field, of Dublin, Cooper; John Harford, of the City of Dublin, Peruke-maker; Benjamin Maddock, of Dublin, Felt-maker; John Winford, of Dublin, Cooper; Ferral Sheridan, of Dublin, Bricklayer; Cornelius Lyne, of Dublin, Vintner; Lewis Ker, Batchelor in Physick; James Sheridan, near Mullingar, Yeoman; Daniel Offlaherty, Merchant; John Ferral, of Dublin, Vintner; Augustine M'Donough, Cook, of Monafter-Evan, in the County of Kildare; Martin O'Connor, of Silver-Mines, in the County of Tipperary, Esquire; Mary Staunton, of Thomas-Street, Widow.

And the following Persons in the Custody of the Marshal of the Marshalsea of the *Four-Courts*:

James Magennis, Miller; James Mullhall, Vintner; Luke Dillon, Vintner; Thomas Quin, Turner; Andrew Clarke, Wine Drawer; Joseph Hamersly, Linen Manufacturer; Ignatius Austin, Shoemaker; John Kenedy, Soldier; Christopher Carpenter, Butcher; Thomas Malone, Sedan Chair-maker; William Ash, Shoemaker; Matthew Quin, Butcher; John Packenham, Labourer; and James Philips, Vintner.

CHAP. XVI. Provided always, That the several Persons mentioned in the said Schedule, may have the full Benefit of this Act, notwithstanding the Sums, in which they are respectively indebted, exceed the Sums herein before mentioned, with respect to Persons who are in actual Custody on the Twenty-fifth Day of October, One thousand seven hundred and sixty.

CHAP. XVII.

AN ACT

FOR

Reviving, Continuing, and Amending several Temporary Statutes, and for other Purposes therein mentioned.

DUBLIN:

Printed by BOULTER GRIERSON, Printer to the King's most Excellent Majesty. MDCCLXII.

(277)

AN ACT FOR

Reviving, Continuing, and Amending several Temporary Statutes, and for other Purposes therein mentioned.

CHAP. XVII.

WHEREAS an Act passed in this Kingdom in the Third Year of the Reign of His late Majesty King George the Second, Intituled, An Act for the further explaining and amending several Statutes for prohibiting Under Sheriffs, and

CHAP. XVII.

Sheriffs Clerks from officiating as Sub-Sheriff or Sheriffs Clerk, more than one Year, and to render more effectual an Act to prevent Fees being taken in certain Cases, and to take away the pretended Office of Barony Clerk, and to oblige Sheriffs to appoint Deputies for granting Replevins, and also for discharging of Prisoners unable to pay their Fees; **Whereby it was, among other Things, Enacted, That so much of the said Act as relates to the preferring of any Bill or Bills in the Courts** of Chancery **or** Exchequer, **for the Discovery of any Offence against the said Act, or against an Act therein mentioned, of the Tenth Year of the Reign of Her late Majesty Queen** Ann, **and as obliges any Person to answer the same at large, without pleading or demurring thereto, should be, and continue in Force, to the First Day of** March, **One thousand seven hundred and Thirty-three, and from thence to the End of the then next Session of Parliament.**

And Whereas the said recited Clause in the said Act, made in the Third Year of the Reign of His said late Majesty, was, from Time to Time, revived, or continued by several subsequent Acts made in this Kingdom, and particularly by an Act made in the Twenty-third Year of the Reign of His said late Majesty, Intituled, An Act for continuing several Temporary Statutes; **but the same**

same hath lately expired; Be it Enacted by the King's Most Excellent Majesty, by and with the Advice and Consent of the Lords Spiritual and Temporal, and Commons in this present Parliament assembled, and by the Authority of the same, That so much of the said Act, made in the Third Year of the Reign of His said late Majesty, as relates to the preferring of any Bill or Bills in the Courts of Chancery or Exchequer, for the Discovery of any Offence against the said Act of the Third Year of the Reign of His said late Majesty, or the said Act of the Tenth Year of the Reign of Her said late Majesty Queen Ann, and as obliges any Person to answer the same at large, without pleading or demurring thereto, shall be revived and continued from the First Day of May, which will be in the Year of our Lord, One thousand seven hundred and sixty-two, for seven Years, and from thence to the End of the then next Session of Parliament, and no longer.

And whereas an Act passed in the Seventeenth Year of the Reign of His late Majesty King George the Second, Intituled, An Act to prevent the pernicious Practice of burning Land, and for the more effectual destroying of Vermin; Which Act, as to such Part thereof, as relates to the burning of Land, by an Act made in the Twenty

CHAP. XVII. first Year of the Reign of His said late Majesty King George the Second, Intituled, An Act for Reviving, Continuing, and Amending, several Temporary Statutes, was continued until the Twenty ninth Day of September, One thousand seven hundred and sixty, and from thence to the End of the then next Session of Parliament; And as to such Part thereof as relates to the giving Rewards for the more effectual destroying of Vermin (excepting Rooks and Herons) was continued to the Twenty-ninth Day of December, One thousand seven hundred and forty nine, and to the End of the then next Session of Parliament. And by another Act, made in the Twenty-third Year of the Reign of His said late Majesty King George the Second, Intituled, An Act for continuing several Temporary Statutes, was further continued for the Space of Four Years, and from thence to the End of the next Session of Parliament, after the Expiration of the said Forty Years; Be it Enacted by the Authority aforesaid, That such Part of the said Act, made in the Seventeenth Year of the Reign of His said late Majesty King George the Second, as relates to the burning of Land, with the following Amendments thereto, shall be made perpetual; and that such Part thereof, as relates to the giving Rewards for the more effectual destroying of Vermin (except Rooks

Rooks and Herons) shall be revived, and shall continue from the First Day of May, which will be in the Year of Our Lord, One thousand seven hundred and sixty-two, to the First Day of May, Which will be in the Year of Our Lord, One thousand seven hundred and sixty-nine, and from thence to the End of the then next Session of Parliament, and no longer.

And Whereas by the said last recited Act, the original Lessors, Where the Soil or Surface is burned, or permitted to be burned by the Occupiers of the Land, and not by the original Lessees, have found great Difficulties in suing for, and recovering the Penalty given by the said Act; Be it Enacted by the Authority aforesaid, That in all Cases Whatsoever, Whether the Soil or Surface shall be burned, or permitted to be burned by the original Lessee or Lessees, or by the Occupier or Occupiers of such Land, and Where the original Lessor is not consenting to such burning, that the original Lessor shall be intitled to recover the Penalty given by the said Act from his immediate Lessee or Lessees, who shall be answerable for the Acts of his or their Under-tenants, and for the Acts of the Occupiers of such Land.

Provided

CHAP. XVII. Provided such original Lessor or Lessors shall commence his or their Suit for the Recovery of the said Penalty, at such next Assizes or Quarter Sessions, as in the said Act is expressed, and such immediate Lessee or Lessees shall and may have the like Remedy over against his Under-tenants, or the Occupiers of such Land so offending, and shall and may recover against them, or any of them, so offending.

Provided that such Suit be commenced at the next Assizes or Quarter Sessions, after such original Lessor shall have so obtained a Decree against such his immediate Lessee or Lessees: And in Case the original Lessor shall not sue for the said Penalty at the next Assizes or Quarter Sessions, as mentioned in the said Act, then it shall and may be lawful for the immediate Lessor or Lessors of the Occupiers of the Land, Who shall burn, or permit to be burned, the Soil or Surface of any Land, to sue for, and recover from such Occupier or Occupiers the said Penalty.

Provided such Suit be commenced at the second Assizes or Quarter Sessions, after the said Land shall be so burned, and that

that the said Assizes or Quarter Sessions shall not be so near, that a Process cannot be served time enough for that Purpose; and in such Cases, the Suit shall be commenced at the next immediate Assizes, or Sessions following.

And Whereas to evade the said Penalty, and to render the Surveying of such Lands, so burned, difficult and expensive, the Persons so offending often leave narrow Ridges or Paths unburned, intermixed with the Paths so burned, by Means whereof, Landlords have been deterred from suing for the said Penalty; for Remedy whereof, Be it further Enacted and Declared by the Authority aforesaid, That all such Ridges or Paths, so left unburned or intermixed with the Parts so burned, shall and may be surveyed in one common Survey, with the other Part or Parts that shall be so burned, and that they shall and may be deemed and considered as Part of the Land so burned, so far as to subject the Person or Persons so offending, to the Penalty in the said Act mentioned, equally as if no such Ridges or Paths had been so left unburned.

And

CHAP. XVII. **And Whereas a Doubt hath arisen, Whether the Penalty for burning the Soil or Surface as aforesaid, was recoverable under the said Act, Where the Quantity of the Soil or Surface, so burned, was** not a full English **Statute Acre; Be it Enacted by the Authority aforesaid, That the Penalty on the Person or Persons so offending, shall be proportioned to the Quantity burnt, though it be under one** English **Statute Acre.**

And Whereas an Act passed in this Kingdom, in the Eleventh Year of the Reign of His late Majesty King George the Second, **Intituled,** An Act for the buying and selling of all Sorts of Corn and Meal, and other Things therein mentioned, by Weight, and for the more effectual preventing the Frauds committed in the buying and selling thereof, and for regulating the Price and Assize of Bread, and for better regulating the Markets, **which said Act was continued and amended by an Act made in the Nineteenth Year of His said late Majesty's Reign, Intituled,** An Act for amending and continuing an Act, **Intituled,** An Act for the buying and selling all Sorts of Corn and Meal, and other Things therein mentioned, by Weight, and for the more effectual preventing Frauds committed in the buying and selling

Georgii Tertii Regis.

ing thereof, and for regulating the Price and Affize of Bread, and for the better regulating the Markets.

And whereas the said last recited Acts having expired, the same were revived with Alterations, Amendments, and Additions thereto, by an Act made in the Twenty-ninth Year of the Reign of His late Majesty King George the Second, Intituled, An Act for reviving and amending an Act paffed in the Eleventh Year of His said late Majesty's Reign, Intituled, An Act for buying and selling all Sorts of Corn and Meal, and other Things therein mentioned, by Weight, and for the more effectual preventing the Frauds committed in the buying and selling thereof, and for regulating the Price and Affize of Bread, and for better regulating the Markets; as also one other Act made in the Nineteenth Year of His said late Majesty's Reign, Intituled, An Act for continuing and amending an Act for buying and selling of all Sorts of Corn and Meal, and other Things therein mentioned, by Weight, and for the more effectual preventing the Frauds committed in the buying and selling thereof, and for regulating the Price and Affize of Bread, and for better regulating the Markets, so far as the said Acts relate to the regulating the Price and Affize of Bread, and the better regulating

CHAP. XVII. regulating the Markets, **which said several Acts are now expired.**

Be it Enacted by the Authority aforesaid, That the said recited Acts of the Eleventh Year of His said late Majesty King George **the Second's Reign, and the Nineteenth Year of His said late Majesty's Reign, and the Twenty-ninth Year of His said late Majesty's Reign, so far only as the said Acts relate to the buying and selling of all Sorts of Corn and Meal, and other Things therein mentioned, by Weight, and for the more effectual preventing the Frauds committed in the buying and selling thereof, shall be made perpetual.**

And be it further Enacted by the Authority aforesaid, That one other Act passed in this Kingdom, in the Sixth Year of the Reign of His late Majesty King George **the First, Intituled,** An Act for the more effectual preventing the ingrossing and regrating of Coals in this Kingdom, **and which is expired, as far as the same is not altered by one other Act made in this Kingdom, in the Thirty-first Year of the Reign of His late Majesty King** George **the Second, Intituled,** An Act to prevent unlawful Combinations to raise the Price of Coals in the City of *Dublin*, **and also so far as the same is not altered by any other Act made in this Kingdom**

Kingdom in this present Session of Parliament, shall be made perpetual.

And be it further Enacted by the Authority aforesaid, That one other Act passed in this Kingdom, in the Fifth Year of His said late Majesty King George the Second's Reign, Intituled, An Act for the better Regulation and Government of Seamen in the Merchants Service, shall be revived and continued in full Force until the First Day of May, Which will be in the Year of Our Lord, One thousand seven hundred and sixty-seven, and from thence to the End of the then next Session of Parliament, and no longer.

And be it further Enacted by the Authority aforesaid, That one other Act passed in this Kingdom, in the Twenty-ninth Year of His said late Majesty King George the Second's Reign, Intituled, An Act for the better regulating Juries, shall be revived and continued in full Force unto the First Day of May, Which shall be in the Year of Our Lord, One thousand seven hundred and seventy-one, and from thence to the End of the then next Session of Parliament, and no longer.

And Whereas it is very difficult, as the Law now stands, to obtain impartial Tryals

CHAP. XVII.

Tryals in Cities, in Cases where the Right to Tolls, Duties, or Customs, claimed by the respective Corporations of such Cities come in Question; Be it Enacted by the Authority aforesaid, That no Issue shall hereafter be tried by a Jury of any City, in any Action or Suit concerning any Tolls, Duties, or Customs, claimed by the Corporation of such City, but every such Issue shall be tried by a Jury of an indifferent County, to be appointed by the Court in which such Action or Suit shall depend.

And be it further Enacted by the Authority aforesaid, That an Act passed in this Kingdom, in the Twenty-fifth Year of the Reign of His said late Majesty King George the Second, Intituled, An Act for the better Preservation of the Game, shall be revived, and continue in full Force until the First Day of May, which shall be in the Year of Our Lord, One thousand seven hundred and sixty-nine, and from thence to the End of the then next Session of Parliament, and no longer.

And be it further Enacted by the Authority aforesaid, That one other Act passed in this Kingdom, in the Fifteenth Year of the Reign of His late Majesty King George the Second, Intituled, An Act for the

the more effectual securing the Payment of Rents, and preventing Frauds by Tenants, which Act was continued by an Act passed in the Twenty-ninth Year of His said Majesty's Reign, and is now expired, shall be revived, and made perpetual.

CHAP. XVII.

And be it further Enacted by the Authority aforesaid, That one other Act passed in this Kingdom, in the Tenth Year of His late Majesty King George the First's Reign, Intituled, An Act for continuing and amending an Act for better regulating the Parish Watches, and amending Highways in this Kingdom, and for preventing the Misapplication of Publick Money; and also for Establishing a Regular Watch in the City of *Dublin*, and to prevent Mischiefs which may happen by Graving in the River *Liffey*; Which Act, as to such part thereof as relates to Parish Watches and Highways in this Kingdom, was continued by an Act passed in the Twenty-ninth Year of His late Majesty King George the Second's Reign, Intituled, An Act for continuing and reviving several Temporary Statutes, and other Purposes therein mentioned; and which is now expired, shall be revived and continued for the Term of Seven Years, from the First Day of May, One thousand seven hundred and sixty-two, and from thence to the End of the then next Session of Parliament.

CHAP. XVII. **And be it further Enacted by the Authority afore said, That one other Act, passed in this Kingdom, in the Ninth Year of His late Majesty King** George the Second, **Intituled,** An Act to prevent the Evil arising by the Retailers of Beer, Ale, Brandy, Rum, Geneva, *Aqua Vitæ*, and other Spirituous Liquors, giving Credit to Servants, Day-Labourers, and other Persons who usually Work, or Ply for Hire or Wages; **Which Act was continued for Fourteen Years, by an Act passed in the Nineteenth Year of His said late Majesty's Reign, Intituled,** An Act for reviving and continuing several Temporary Statutes, **and Which Act is now expired, shall be revived and made perpetual; Be it further Enacted by the Authority aforesaid, That one other Act, passed in this Kingdom, in the Twenty-ninth Year of the Reign of His said late Majesty King** George the Second, **Intituled,** An Act to prevent unlawful Combinations of Tenants, Colliers, Miners, and others, and the sending of threatning Letters, without Names, or with fictitious Names subscribed thereunto, and the malicious setting Fire to Houses or Out-houses, or to Stacks of Hay, Corn, Straw, or Turf, or to Ships, or Boats, **and Which Act is now near expiring, shall be made perpetual.**

And

And Whereas, notwithstanding the said Act, many Frauds are committed by Colliers, Miners, Carmen, Buyers of Coals, and others; For Remedy whereof, Be it Enacted by the Authority aforesaid, That from and after the first Day of May, One thousand seven hundred and sixty-two, every Carman, and Buyer of Coals, at or in any Colliery of this Kingdom, shall, at the Time of buying said Coal, and before he shall take or remove said Coal from the Place of Sale, procure a Ticket from the Owner of such Coal, or the Clerk, or Person who shall be appointed by the Owner to sell or deliver such Coal, which Ticket shall be given gratis to such Carman or Buyer, and shall express the Day of the Month and Year, in which such Coal is sold and delivered, and also the Quantity of the Coal then sold, and the Names of the Buyer and Seller; and in case any Carman, or Buyer of Coals, or any other Person, shall, after the First Day of May aforesaid, remove or take away any Quantity of Coals from any Colliery, without such Ticket, or shall refuse to produce or shew such Ticket, when required of him, within the said Colliery, or Five Miles thereof, such Person or Persons so offending, shall not only forfeit the Coals so found on him or them, but shall also forfeit the Horse and

**C H A P.
XVII.**

CHAP. XVII.

and Cart employed in carrying such Coal, which Forfeiture shall be to the Use of the Owner or Proprietor of such Colliery, from which such Coal was so taken away. And it is hereby provided, That if any Person, who shall fairly buy any Quantity of Coals, shall, by any Accident lose his Ticket, and for want of such Ticket, shall incur the Penalty herein before mentioned, such Person, shewing by the Clerk of the Colliery's Books, or by proper and sufficient Proof, before the next Justice of Peace, that such Coal was fairly and openly purchased from the Owner or Person appointed to sell the same, shall have his Coal, together with his Horse and Cart restored to him.

And be it further Enacted by the Authority aforesaid, That if any Miner, Master, or other Collier, or other Person employed in any of the Collieries or Mines of this Kingdom, shall, from and after the first Day of May, One thousand seven hundred and sixty-two, absent himself from his Work, in Breach of his Articles or Contract with the Owner or Owners of any Colliery, or other Mine, or shall engage himself, or hire with the Owner or Owners, Overseer or Director of any other Colliery or Mine, or any other Person whatsoever, without first obtaining a Licence, or Discharge in Writing, from the Owner or Owners of the last Work he was

was engaged by Contract or Agreement to Work in, such Miner, Master, or other Collier, on being Duly convicted of such Offence, shall, over and above the Penalties provided by any former Act, be committed to the Common Goal of the County wherein such Offence is committed, there to remain for the Space of Two Months, without Bail or Mainprize. And if any Owner of any Colliery or Mine, shall employ or hire any such Miner, Master, or other Collier under Contract, as herein before mentioned, who shall not obtain such Licence or Discharge in Writing, and produce the same before he shall be so hired or employed, such Owner of a Mine, or Colliery, so offending, for such Offence shall, over and above all the other Penalties by any former Act or Acts, forfeit or pay the Sum of Ten Pounds, to such Owner from whom such Miner, Master, or other Collier shall be so seduced, to be recovered by Civil Bill, at the Assizes to be held for the County where such Offence shall be committed. And if any other Person or Persons Whatsoever, shall employ or hire any Miner, Master, or other Collier, under Contract as herein before mentioned, knowing him to be such, without a Licence or Discharge obtained, and produced as herein before mentioned, such

4 E   Person

CHAP. XVII. Person or Persons so offending, shall likewise forfeit the Sum of Ten Pounds, to be recovered in the Manner herein before mentioned, said Sum, so forfeited, to be paid to the Master or Owner of the Colliery from whom such Miner, Master, or other Collier shall be so seduced.

Provided always, and be it Enacted by the Authority aforesaid, That the said two Clauses herein before last mentioned, shall continue and be in Force, to the first Day of May, which shall be in the Year of Our Lord, One thousand seven hundred and sixty-four, and to the End of the then next Session of Parliament, and no longer.

And Whereas by an Act made in the Tenth Year of the Reign of King George the First, it is Enacted, That every Weigh-Master to be appointed in Pursuance of the said Act, should provide convenient Weigh-Houses in each City.

And Whereas there is but one Weigh-House at present in the City of Limerick, and that situated in a very inconvenient Place, which is a great Obstruction to the Trade of the said City; Be it Enacted by the Authority aforesaid, That the Weigh-Master of the said City of Limerick, shall, before

before the First Day of May, One thousand seven hundred and sixty-three, provide Two convenient Weigh-Houses for the said City, One to be in the English Town, the other in the Irish Town of the said City, in some convenient Places, to be approved of by the Majority of the Wholesale Merchants of the said City.

CHAP. XVII.

And whereas an Act passed in the Sixth Year of the Reign of His late Majesty King George the First, Intituled, An Act for erecting and continuing Lights in the City of *Dublin*, and the several Liberties adjoining, and also in the Cities of *Cork* and *Limerick*, and Liberties thereof; Which said Act was amended by an Act made in the Eighth Year of His said late Majesty's Reign, Intituled, An Act for amending an Act, Intituled, An Act for erecting and continuing Lights in the City of *Dublin*, and the several Liberties adjoining; and also in the Cities of *Cork* and *Limerick*, and Liberties thereof; and the same was explained and amended by another Act, made in the Third Year of the Reign of His late Majesty King George the Second, Intituled, An Act for explaining and amending an Act, made in the Sixth Year of the Reign of His late Majesty King *George* the First, Intituled, An Act for erecting and continuing Lights in the City of *Dublin*, and the several Liberties adjoining

CHAP. XVII.
ing, and also in the Cities of *Cork* and *Limerick*, and Liberties thereof.

And Whereas an Act passed in the Fifteenth Year of the Reign of His said late Majesty, Intituled, An Act to revive and amend an Act, made in the Sixth Year of His said late Majesty King *George* the First, for erecting and continuing Lights in the City of *Dublin*, and the several Liberties adjoining; and also in the Cities of *Cork* and *Limerick*, and Liberties thereof, as far as the same relates to the Liberties adjoining to the City of *Dublin*, and to the Cities of *Cork* and *Limerick*, and Liberties thereof; Which said Acts are now near expiring, but some Parts thereof being found useful, are thought fit to be continued; Be it therefore Enacted by the Authority aforesaid, That all and every Clause, Article, and Proviso in the said Acts contained, touching, and in respect of the Liberties of Sepulchre's, Thomas Court, and Donore, shall remain and be in full Force and Effect as they now stand, to all Intents and Purposes, for the Space of Twenty-one Years, to commence from the First Day of May, which shall be in the Year of our Lord, One thousand seven hundred and Sixty-three, and to the End of the then next Session of Parliament.

And

Georgii Tertii Regis.

CHAP. XVII.

And Whereas several **Acts for erecting** and continuing **Lights** in several **Cities** and **Towns-Corporate**, are near expiring.

And Whereas an Act passed the last Session of Parliament, Intituled, An Act for the more effectual enlighting the City of *Dublin*, and the Liberties thereof; and for the erecting of Publick Lights in the other Cities, Towns-Corporate, and Market-Towns in this Kingdom.

And Whereas a Doubt may arise, whether, after the Expiration of the said first recited Acts, the last recited Act will extend to such Cities and Towns-Corporate, for which Provision had been before made by the said first recited Acts; Be it Enacted by the Authority aforesaid, That from and immediately after the Expiration of the said respective first recited Acts, all the Clauses and Provisoes in the said last recited Act contained, except such as relate only to the City of Dublin, **and the Liberties thereof, shall extend to the several Cities and Towns-Corporate, in the said first recited Act mentioned.**

And Whereas by the Charters of several Boroughs and Corporations in this Kingdom, certain Oaths are required to be taken by the several Officers and Members

Chap. of such Boroughs and Corporations, in
XVII. the Presence of, and to be administred by
the Persons in such Charters respectively
mentioned.

And whereas several Officers and Members of such Boroughs and Corporations, though they have been duly Elected, and though they have taken the several Oaths required by the said respective Charters, are nevertheless subject to Prosecutions, by reason that the several Requisites, directed by the said Charters, have not been observed at the Swearing of such Officers and Members.

For Remedy whereof, and for the more effectual quieting such Corporations, Be it Enacted by the Authority aforesaid, That no Person who hath been duly Elected into any such Office or Franchise, shall hereafter be ousted out of any such Office or Franchise, in any Ways sued, molested, or prosecuted, for or upon account of any Objection which shall or may be taken to the Swearing such Officers or Members, provided that such Officers and Members shall, in fact, have taken the Oaths required by Law; and such Officers and Members shall be deemed legal Officers and Members of such Boroughs and Corporations, and all Corporate Acts which
have

have been done by them, shall have the same C H A P.
Force and Effect, as if such Officers and XVII.
Members had been respectively sworn, pursuant to the Directions of the said respective Charters.

And Whereas an Act passed in the Thirty-third Year of His late Majesty's Reign, Intituled, An Act for the more equal Assessing, and better Collecting of Publick Money, in Counties of Cities, and Counties of Towns, is near expiring, and is fit to be continued, with the Amendments herein after mentioned; Be it Enacted by the Authority aforesaid, That in case any of the Ministers in the said recited Act mentioned, or their Curates, shall refuse or neglect to summon or hold Vestries, within the Time prescribed by the said Act, for the Purpose of applotting the Money to be raised in their respective Parishes, or shall refuse or neglect to return such Applotments, as by the said Act is directed, every such Minister, in whose Parish there shall be such Neglect, shall forfeit, for every such Offence, the Sum of Ten Pounds, to be recovered by Civil Bill, before the Judges of Assize, by any Person who shall sue for the same. And in case any of the Treasurers, in the said Act mentioned, shall refuse or neglect to collect the several Sums, presented and applotted in pursuance of the said Act, before the Assizes

4 F 2   next

CHAP. XVII.

next ensuing the Assizes at which the same shall have been presented, and it shall appear to such Judge or Judges of Assize, that such Neglect was wilful, it shall and may be lawful to and for such Judge or Judges of Assize, to fine such Treasurer in any Sum, not exceeding the Sum of Twenty Pounds, and to commit him for the same.

And be it Enacted by the Authority aforesaid, That the said recited Act, with the Alterations and Amendments herein contained, shall be continued from the Twenty fifth Day of March, One thousand seven hundred and sixty-two, for the Term of Twenty-one Years, and from thence to the End of the then next Session of Parliament.

Provided always, That nothing in the said Act, or herein contained, shall extend to the Cities, or Counties of the Cities of Dublin or Cork.

And Whereas great Abuses have prevailed in Cities and Towns-Corporate in this Kingdom, by the exacting of several unreasonable and excessive Tolls of Corn, Grain, and other Goods and Merchandizes, not warranted by Law, Charter, or Usage;

For

For Remedy whereof, Be it Enacted by the Authority aforesaid, That the Mayor, or other Chief Magistrate of every City and Town-Corporate, shall cause a Schedule of the Duties, Tolls, or Customs, claimed by the Corporation of such City or Town-Corporate, to be hung up in some conspicuous Part of the Market-House or Market-Houses of such City or Town-Corporate, on every Market-Day, for One Month next ensuing every Michaelmas Day; and in case of Neglect so to do, such Mayor, or other Chief Magistrate, shall, for every such Neglect, forfeit a Penalty of Ten Pounds, Sterling, to be recovered in a Summary Way, by Civil Bill, at the next Assizes, by any Person or Persons who shall sue for the same.

And Be it further Enacted by the Authority aforesaid, That if any Officer of any Corporation, Farmer of Tolls, or Toll-Gatherer, shall exact from, or compel any Person or Persons to pay any Duty, Toll, Custom, or Perquisite, not mentioned or comprized in such Schedule, to be hung up as aforesaid, such Officer, Farmer of Tolls, or Toll-Gatherer, shall, for every such Offence, forfeit the Sum of Five Pounds, Sterling, to be recovered by Civil Bill, at the next Assizes, by any Person, from whom any unlawful Duty, Toll, Custom, or Perquisite, shall be so exacted.

And whereas the Progress of the Linen Manufacture has been in many Places retarded by a Scarcity of Fuel; Be it Enacted by the Authority aforesaid, That all Turf, Furze, and Timber in Faggots, for Fuel, shall pass into and through every City and Town, Free from all Toll, Custom, or Perquisite whatsoever, claimed by any Officer or Member of such City or Town.

And be it further Enacted by the Authority aforesaid, That an Act passed in the Twenty-fifth Year of His late Majesty's Reign, for the better adjusting, and more easy Recovery of the Wages of certain Servants, and certain Apprentices, and for the Punishment of such Owners of Coals, and their Agents, as shall knowingly employ and set at Work Persons retained in the Service of other Owners, and also that mutual Debts between Party and Party be set one against the other, which Act, by an Act passed in the Twenty-ninth Year of His said late Majesty's Reign, for continuing and reviving several Temporary Statutes, and other Purposes therein mentioned, was continued with several Amendments, to the Twenty-fifth Day of March, One thousand seven hundred and sixty, and

to

Georgii Tertii Regis. 303

to the End of the then next Session of Parliament, may be continued for four Years, from the End of this present Session of Parliament, and to the End of the then next Session of Parliament, after the Expiration of the said Term of Four Years.

CHAP. XVII.

CHAP. XVIII.

AN ACT

FOR

The more easy and equal assessing and applotting all Money presented by the Grand Jury of each Assizes to be held for the City and County of the City of *Cork*, and for putting the Coaches, Chaises, Chairs, and Sedans, that ply for Hire in the said City, under the like Regulations, for the Benefit of the Work-house of *Cork*, as they are in *Dublin*; and also for the better regulating the Harbour of *Cork*.

DUBLIN:

Printed by BOULTER GRIERSON, Printer to the King's most Excellent Majesty. MDCCLXII.

(307)

AN ACT

FOR

The more easy and equal assessing and applotting all Money presented by the Grand Jury of each Assizes to be held for the City, and County of the City of *Cork*, and for putting the Coaches, Chaises, Chairs, and Sedans, that ply for Hire in the said City, under the like Regulations, for the Benefit of the Workhouse of *Cork*, as they are in *Dublin*, and also for the better regulating the Harbour of *Cork*.

CHAP. XVIII.

Whereas by an Act made in the Seventeenth Session of his late Majesty King George the Second, Intituled, An Act for the more equal assessing, and collecting and assessing of Publick Money in Counties of Cities, and Counties of Towns, hath

CHAP. XVIII.

been

CHAP. XVIII.

been found ineffectual and insufficient, in several Counties of Cities, for the Purpose thereby intended.

And Whereas the County of the City of Cork, is a very large and extensive County, and contains upwards of Ninety-six Plowlands of uncertain Acreage and Measure; Be it therefore Enacted by the King's most Excellent Majesty, by and with the Advice and Consent of the Lords Spiritual and Temporal, and Commons in this present Parliament assembled, and by the Authority of the same, That from and after the First Day of June, One thousand seven hundred and sixty-two, the Grand Jury of each Assizes to be held for said City, and County of the said City of Cork, shall present Twenty-six Persons out of the Inhabitants of the said City and County, by the Name of Applotters, for assessing and applotting all Publick Money, presented to be raised in the said City, and County of the said City, at the said several Assizes, and that the said Applotters shall severally and respectively make Oath on the Holy Evangelists, equally and impartially, according to the best of their Skill and Knowledge, to applot and assess all Publick Money, so appointed to be raised; and that the Mayor of the said City, for the Time being, may be impowered and required to administer

nister the said Oath, for which Oath, no
Fees shall be taken, and to summon the
said Applotters to appear before him, to
take said Oath.

CHAP.
XVIII.

And be it further Enacted by the Authority aforesaid, That the several and respective High and Petty Constables of the said City, and County of the said City of Cork, shall, within One Kalendar Month, to be computed from the first Day of each Assizes, deliver unto the Mayor of the said City, upon Oath, a true Return in Writing, of the Names and Places of Abode of the several Inhabitants or House-Keepers within their respective Limits, which Oath the said Mayor is hereby impowered to administer, without Fee as aforesaid, and that the Mayor of the said City shall deliver in the said Returns of the said Constables, to any One or more of the said Applotters, at the Time of his and their taking before him the Applotters Oath before mentioned.

And be it further Enacted by the Authority aforesaid, That the said Applotters, or any seven or more of them, shall, within Three Months from the First Day of every Assizes in which such Money shall be appointed to be raised, from Time to Time, Assemble and Meet together, and

CHAP. XVIII. applot and assess such Publick Money on the several Inhabitants and Lands in the said City, and County of the said City, by Thirteen distinct Applotments, for the several Divisions following, into which the said City of Cork hath, for Time immemorial, been divided, and for which Divisions, High and Petty Constables, for Time immemorial, have been distinctly appointed (that is to say) One Applotment for the North Liberties of the said City, a Second for the South Liberties of said City, a Third for the North Suburbs of said City, a Fourth for the South Suburbs of the said City, a Fifth for the North East Quarter of said City, a Sixth for the North West Quarter of said City, a Seventh for the South East Quarter of said City, an Eighth for the South West Quarter of said City, a Ninth for the North East Quarter of the Parish of Saint Mary Shandon in said City, a Tenth for the North West Quarter of the Parish of Saint Mary Shandon in said City, an Eleventh for Mallow Lane, and Fair Lane, in said City, a Twelfth for the Parish of Saint Paul in said City, and a Thirteenth for the Parish of Saint Finbary in said City; and that the said Applotters, or any Seven or more of them, shall make regular and fair Entries of all such Assessments or Applotments, in a Book to be kept by them for that Purpose, and to be

provided

CHAP.
XVIII.

provided for them, by the Treasurer of the said City, and each Distinct Applotment or Assessment to be subscribed with the Names of such Applotters so assembled; and that said Applotters shall ascertain and applot the Sums to be raised upon such Parts of the County of the said City, as have been usually charged, according to the Plow Land, and upon such Parts as have been usually charged, according to the Acre; and as to such Parts of the said City and County thereof, as have been heretofore usually charged, according to the Substance of the Inhabitants, they shall ascertain and applot the Sum to be paid by each Inhabitant; and that the Persons making such Assessments or Applotments respectively, shall, within Ten Days after such Assessments or Applotments being made and signed by them as aforesaid, deliver, or cause to be delivered to the said Treasurer, the said Book, containing the said Assessments or Applotments, and that the Assessments or Applotments contained therein, shall be final and conclusive to all Parties.

And be it further Enacted by the Authority aforesaid, That in case any of the said Applotters shall neglect or refuse to appear before the said Mayor to take the said Applotters Oath, by the Space of Four Days next after his being

CHAP.
XVIII.

ing ferved with the Mayor's Summons for that purpofe, or abfent himfelf from any fuch Affembly, without being able to fhew reafonable Caufe for the fame, fo as that a fufficient Number fhall not meet to affefs fuch Publick Money, every Perfon, fo neglecting or refufing to appear before the faid Mayor, and take faid Oath, or abfenting himfelf, fhall, for every fuch Offence, forfeit the Sum of Ten Pounds, Sterling, to be recovered by Civil Bill, before the next going Judges of Affize for the faid City, and County of the faid City of Cork, by the Treafurer of the faid City; and that the faid Treafurer may be authorized and required to fue for the fame, and that the Money fo recovered, fhall be accounted for by the faid Treafurer, at the next enfuing Affizes, as part of the Publick Money.

And be it further Enacted by the Authority aforefaid, That the feveral Conftables of the faid feveral Divifions of the faid City, and County of the faid City, fhall, within their refpective Limits, collect, by Warrant under the Hand and Seal of the faid Treafurer, Which Warrant the faid Treafurer is hereby impowered to grant, the feveral Sums fo prefented and applotted, as aforefaid, and fhall pay in the faid feveral Sums to the faid Treafurer, before the

Affizes

Assizes next ensuing the said Assizes at which the same shall be so presented; and that the said Treasurer shall, at every Assizes, make up his Accounts, upon Oath, of all his Receipts and Payments of the said Publick Money so received by him, and shall return, and lay the said Accounts, fairly Written, with the Affidavit of the said Treasurer at the Foot thereof, taken before the Judge of Assize, without Fee, verifying the Truth of such Accounts, on the first Day of every Assizes, before the Grand Jury of the said City, to be viewed, allowed, or disapproved of by the said Grand Jury; and that the said Grand Jury shall cause the same to be entered in the Book of the County of the said City, with such Observations as they shall think fit; and in Default of such Return, that it shall and may be lawful for the respective Judges of Assize, to fine such Treasurer, in any Sum not exceeding the Sum so presented and applotted as aforesaid, and to commit such Treasurer in Execution for the same.

And be it further Enacted by the Authority aforesaid, That if any of the said Constables shall neglect, omit, or refuse to make the aforesaid Returns to the Mayor of the said City, or to collect the Sums so presented and applotted, or to pay in the same to the Treasurer of the said City,

within

CHAP. XVIII.

Within the Time herein before appointed for that Purpose, it shall and may be lawful to and for the respective Judges of Assize, to fine the said Constables so neglecting, omitting, or refusing to make the said Return, in any Sum not exceeding Ten Pounds, and to commit such Offenders in Execution for the same; and for omitting, neglecting, or refusing to collect the Sums so presented and applotted, or to pay in the same to the Treasurer, in such Sum or Sums of Money, as to the said Judges shall seem proper, not exceeding the Sums that such Constables shall by the Warrants of the said Treasurer be appointed respectively to receive, and to commit the said several Offenders in Execution for the same.

And be it further Enacted by the Authority aforesaid, That in case the Occupier or Occupiers of the said several Houses and Lands in the said City, and County of the said City, shall refuse to pay the Sum or Sums so applotted and assessed, it shall and may be lawful to and for the said several Constables, within their respective Limits, by Warrant under the Hand and Seal of the said Treasurer (Oath being first made by the Constable or Constables, of his or their having made a Demand of the said Sum or Sums so appplotted or assessed,

CHAP.
XVIII.

fessed, and of the same being refused to be paid, for the Space of Five Days after Demand so made, which Oath the said Treasurer is hereby impowered, to administer (without Fee) to distrain the Goods and Chattels of the Person or Persons so refusing, and to sell the same by Publick Cant on the Fifth Day after the taking the said Distress, for the Payment and Discharge of the said respective Sum or Sums so assessed, unless paid within the said Time, rendering the Overplus (if any be) to the Owners.

And whereas several Sums of Money were, at the several late Assizes held for the County of the said City (to wit) at the several Assizes held for the County of the said City, on the Twenty-seventh of March, One thousand seven hundred and sixty; on the Seventh of August, One thousand seven hundred and sixty; and on the Twenty-seventh of March, One thousand seven hundred and sixty-one, presented by the respective Grand Juries of the said several Assizes, to be raised for the Purposes in the said Presentments, respectively mentioned.

And whereas the Grand Jury of the said City, at the next Lent Assizes to be held for the County of the said City, may present several further Sums of Money to be raised in the County of the said City.

4 K 2   And

CHAP.
XVIII.
And whereas the Sums, so already presented to be raised at the said Three former Assizes, or to be presented to be raised at the said next Lent Assizes, cannot, for want of being properly applotted, be collected or raised; Be it therefore further Enacted by the Authority aforesaid, That the several Sums, so presented to be raised, at the said Three former Assizes, or to be presented to be raised at the next Lent Assizes, shall, within Three Months after the next Summer Assizes to be holden for the County of the said City, be equally and impartially assessed by the Applotters, or any Five or more of them, to be nominated at the said next Summer Assizes, in Manner herein before appointed; and that the said several Sums shall be collected, raised, and paid in such Manner, and with such Remedy and Powers as are herein before contained, for applotting and raising all Publick Money to be presented, to be raised at every Assizes to be holden for the said City, and County of the said City of Cork, from and after the said First Day of June, One thousand seven hundred and sixty-two.

And be it further Enacted by the Authority aforesaid, That if any Suit shall be commenced against any Person or Persons for any Act done in pursuance of this Act,

the

the Defendant may plead the General Issue, and give the Special Matter in Evidence; and that if a Verdict be given for the Defendant, or the Plaintiff become nonsuited, or discontinue his Action, the Defendant shall have double Cost.

CHAP. XVIII.

And be it further Enacted by the Authority aforesaid, That so much of this Act, as is herein before contained, shall remain and be in Force for Two Years, from the First Day of June, One thousand seven hundred and sixty-two, and from thence to the End of the next Sessions of Parliament, and no longer.

And Whereas several Persons have, for some Years past, kept Hackney Coaches, Post Chaises, Chairs and Sedans, to ply for Hire within the said City of Cork, and the Liberties thereto adjoining.

And Whereas the regulating the Rates and Fares, of the said Hackney Coaches, Post Chaises, Chairs and Sedans, and of the Drivers and Carriers of the same, within the said City and Liberties, will prevent many Impositions being made on the Inhabitants of the said City and Liberties, and will tend to provide for the Uses of the Workhouse established in said City; Be it Enacted by the Authority aforesaid, That from and after

after the First Day of June, One thousand seven hundred and sixty-two, the Governors of the Work-House of the said City of Cork, Fifteen at least being present, shall and may be authorized and required, under their Common Seal, to licence for the Term of Twenty-one Years, from the said First Day of June, One thousand seven hundred and sixty-two, all such Person or Persons as shall keep, drive, or carry any Hackney Coaches, Post-Chaises, Chairs, or Sedans, plying for Hire within the said City of Cork, or Liberties thereto adjoining, and from Time to Time to limit the Number of such Coaches, Post-Chaises, Chairs, and Sedans, as the said Governors shall think proper; and that the Governors of the said Work-House shall, for every Licence to be granted for each Coach and Post-Chaise, be paid the Sum of Twenty Shillings, by Way of Fine, before such Licence shall be delivered; and that upon every Licence for each Coach or Post-Chaise, there shall be reserved to the Governors of the said Work-house, and their Successors, the yearly Rent of Twenty Shillings, and for each Chair or Sedan, Ten Shillings, to be paid Quarterly, on every First Day of September, First Day of December, First Day of March, and First Day of May, in every Year, with such Covenants therein to be inserted, for the more effectual Payment thereof,

thereof, as the said Governors, or any Fifteen or more of them, shall think fit; and
that no Person shall keep, drive, carry, or let
to Hire, any Coach, Post-Chaise, Chair, or
Sedan, to ply within the said City or Liberties, without such Licence first obtained,
under the Penalty of Ten Pounds for
every Coach or Post-Chaise, and Five
Pounds for every Chair or Sedan, which
shall so ply, contrary to this Act; and that
every Coach, Post-Chaise, Chair, or Sedan,
so to be licenced, shall have a Mark of Distinction, by a Figure on a large Brass
Plate, with the Number in large Figures,
and that the said Mark shall be placed on
each side of every such Coach, Post-Chaise,
Chair, or Sedan, in such Manner as the
said Governors shall think proper, and that
every Coachman, Driver, Chairman, or
Carriers of any Coach, Post-Chaise, Chair,
or Sedan, plying for Hire as aforesaid, who
shall drive or carry, without such Mark of
Distinction or Figure, any Coach, Post-
Chaise, Chair, or Sedan, or if any Person
shall blot out, deface, or change the Mark or
Figure appointed for such Coach, Post-
Chaise, Chair, or Sedan, every Person so
offending, for every such Offence shall forfeit Thirty Shillings; and that the said
Sums so to be paid for Licences, and the
yearly Rents to be reserved therein, and also
the aforesaid several Penalties, shall go,
and

Chap. XVIII. go, and be paid to the Treasurer of the said Work-house, for the Use of the said Work-house; and that the said several Penalties aforesaid, and also the several Penalties and Forfeitures herein after mentioned, shall and may be recovered before the Governors of the said Work-house, or before Five or more of them, in a summary Way, on Proof being made before them on Oath, after one Summons, to the Party offending, and shall be levied by Distress and Sale of the Offenders Goods and Chattles, by Warrant under the Hand and Seal of such Governors, or any Five or more of them, unless such Penalty be paid within Ten Days after such Distress be taken, and that the Overplus (if any be) all Charges being deducted, be paid to the Owner; and that in Case no sufficient Distress can be had to answer the said Penalties respectively, the Person and Persons so offending, shall, by Warrant under the Hand and Seal of the said Governors, or any Five or more of them, be sent to the House of Correction, there to be kept to hard Labour, for any Time not exceeding One Month.

And be it further Enacted by the Authority aforesaid, That all Licences so to be granted for Coaches, Post Chaises, Chairs or Sedans, shall be granted for the Term of of Twenty-one Years, from the said First Day of June, One thousand seven hundred and sixty-two, and shall be deviseable or transferable by the Parties to whom the same shall be granted, their Executors, Administrators, or Assigns, under the Rents and Covenants therein contained.

Provided always, and be it further Enacted by the Authority aforesaid, That no Person who shall be possessed of a Licence for keeping a Chair or Sedan for Hire, shall transfer or assign the same, without the Consent of the said Governors, or Five or more of them, first had in Writing under their Hands and Seals; and that if any Person or Persons to be possessed of any such Licence or Licences for keeping a Chair or Sedan for Hire, shall transfer the same, without the Consent of the said Governors, or Five of them, signified as aforesaid, every such Transfer shall be void, and that every Licence so assigned, shall be forfeited to the said Governors, for the Use of the said Work-house.

And be it further Enacted by the Authority aforesaid, That it shall and may be lawful, to and for the Governors of the said Work-house, Fifteen at least being present, under their common Seal, from Time to Time, to settle and adjust the several

veral Rates, Fares and Prices, to be paid to the respective Drivers of the said Hackney Coaches or Post Chaises, and the Carriers of the said Chairs or Sedans, for the Hire of such Coaches, Post Chaises, Chairs or Sedans, by the Day or Hour, or by the Set-down, to or from any Part or Parts within the said City, or within the Liberties to the said City adjoining, and to adjudge the several Distances within the said City and Liberties, for which the said Rates, Fares and Prices shall be paid, and also to make Orders and By Laws, to bind all and every Person and Persons, who shall have Licences to keep Hackney Coaches, Post Chaises, Chairs or Sedans for Hire as aforesaid, and all Coach-men, Post Chaise-men, Chair-men, Drivers and Carriers thereof, and to annex such reasonable Penalties and Forfeitures, not exceeding Forty Shillings for the Breach of any such By Law, or Order, on the several Persons offending, or by making void the Licence the Person so offending had, or by subjecting the several Persons so offending to corporal Punishment, by sending him or them to the House of Correction, there to be Whipped and kept to hard Labour, for any Time not exceeding Ten Days, and that the said Governors, or any Five or more of them, shall and may, by Warrant under their Hands and

and Seals, put the said By-Laws and Orders, by the said Governors, or any Fifteen or more of them, so to be made, into due Execution, according to the Tenor and Effect of the said By-Law, and Orders, so as such Rates, Fairs and Prices, and such Rules, Orders and By-Laws, shall be first approved of by the then next going Judges of Assize for the County of the said City, under their respective Hands and Seals, and that after such Approbation, the said Rates, Fairs and Prices, and the said Rules, Orders, and By-Laws, shall be printed, and publickly posted on the Tholsel of the said City of Cork, and on the said Work-house, and such other Places as the said Governors shall appoint, and shall from thenceforth be valid and effectual.

And be it further Enacted by the Authority aforesaid, That from and after the Time the said Rates, Fares and Prices shall be so limited and approved of as aforesaid, no Hackney Coach-man, Post Chaise-man, Driver, or Carrier, of any Hackney Coach, Post Chaise, Chair, or Sedan, in or about the said City, or within the Liberties thereof, shall take by the Day, Hour, or Set-down, above the Rates, Fares, and Prices, so to be limited as aforesaid, and that if any Coach-man, Post Chaise-man,

CHAP.
XVIII.

Chaise-man, Chair-man, or Carriers of Chairs or Sedans, shall exact more for his Fare than according to the several Rates so to be limited, or behave with Insolence to his Fare, or leave his Fare without Permission, the Owners of such Coach, Post Chaise, Chair, or Sedan, shall for every such Offence of such Coach-man, Post Chaise-man, Chair-man, or Carriers of Chairs or Sedans, forfeit any Sum not exceeding Forty Shillings, to be levied or applied in Manner as is herein before directed.

And be it further Enacted by the Authority aforesaid, That if any Person or Persons shall refuse to pay any Coach-man, Post Chaise-man, Driver, or Carriers of any Chairs or Sedans, the Money justly due to him for carrying such Person or Persons in his Coach, Post Chaise, Chair, or Sedan, or shall wilfully break or deface any such Coach, Post Chaise, Chair, or Sedan, it shall and may be lawful, to and for the said Governors, or any Two or more of them, upon Complaint made, and after one Summons directed by them to the Party or Parties complained against, finally to hear and determine the Matter complained of, and upon Proof made thereof upon Oath, by one credible Witness, or by Confession of the Party,

to

to aford a reasonable Satisfaction to the Party aggrieved, for his Damage and Costs, to be levied upon Refusal, to make such Satisfaction by Warrant under the Hands and Seals of the said Governors, or any Two or more of them, by Distress and Sale of the Offenders Goods, rendering the Overplus (if any be) to the Owners.

And whereas the Advancement and Improvement of Navigation, within the Harbour of the said City of Cork, will conduce to the publick Benefit of this Kingdom: Wherefore, and for the preventing the Channel of the River Lee, within the said Harbour, from being choked or impaired, and also for the preventing Disputes between Masters, Owners, and Freighters of Ships within the said Harbour; Be it Enacted by the Authority aforesaid, That from and after the First Day of June, One thousand seven hundred and sixty-two, no Ship, Bark, Boat, or other Vessel, having Ballast to discharge within the Harbour of the said City of Cork, shall discharge the same, or any Part thereof, in the said River Lee, but in such Place or Places as shall be appointed by the Water Bailiff of the said City, or his Deputy, unless the same be discharged above High Water Mark, under the Penalty

Chap. XVIII.
nalty and Forfeiture of Twenty Shillings for each Vessel of the Burthen of Twenty Tuns or upwards, and the Penalty and Forfeiture of Ten Shillings, for each Vessel under the Burthen of Twenty Tuns.

And be it further Enacted by the Authority aforesaid, That from and after the Time aforesaid, every Ship, Bark, Boat, or other Vessel, taking in Ballast from any Lighter or other Vessel, or discharging Ballast into any Lighter, or other Vessel, within the said Harbour, shall nail or fix a Tarpaulin or Sail Cloth from the Gunnel or Ballast Port of such Vessel, to hang over the Gunnel of such Lighter or other Vessel, so as to prevent any Ballast or Dirt falling into the said River, under the Penalty and Forfeiture of Ten Shillings for each such Offence.

And be it further Enacted by the Authority aforesaid, That from and after the Time aforesaid, no Ship, Bark, Boat, or other Vessel, shall take up any Ballast or Filling in any Part of the said River Lee, below the North and South Bridges of the said City of Cork, except in such Place or Places, as shall, from Time to Time, be appointed by the said Water-Bailiff, or his Deputy, under the like Penalty and Forfeiture

feiture of Ten Shillings, for every such Offence.

And be it further Enacted by the Authority aforesaid, That from and after the Time aforesaid, no Person shall throw any Stones, Rubbish, or Dirt, into the said River, or into any other Publick Docks or Creeks of the said River, and that every Person offending therein, shall forfeit, for every such Offence, Two Shillings and Sixpence, and that such Stones, Rubbish, or Dirt, shall be removed out of the said River, Channel, Dock, or Creek, at the Costs and Charges of the Offender.

And be it further Enacted by the Authority aforesaid, That from and after the Time aforesaid, every Ship, or other Vessel, anchoring or mooring in the said River, between the Spit End and Dundaniel House, shall keep proper and sufficient Buoys to their Anchors, in Order to prevent other Ships from mooring foul, or overlaying each other; and that every Master, or other Person, who shall have Charge of a Ship, or other Vessel, who shall Offend herein, shall, for every such Offence, forfeit Ten Shillings.

CHAP. XVIII. And be it further Enacted by the Authority aforesaid, That from and after the Time aforesaid, every Ship, or other Vessel, anchoring or mooring in the said River, from Dundaniel-House to the Marsh-End, shall carry their Anchors as far out of the Channel, as may be conveniently done, and shall also keep proper and sufficient Buoys to their Anchors, and that every Ship, or other Vessel, anchoring or mooring from the Marsh-End to the Custom-House Dock in the said City of Cork, shall carry their Anchors to the Southward of the Channel, beyond low Water Mark, and shall also keep proper and sufficient Buoys to their Anchors; and that every Ship or other Vessel, anchoring or mooring in the said River, from the Custom-House Dock to the North Bridge in the said City, shall place their Anchor as far from the Center as possible, and shall also keep proper and suficient Buoys to their Anchors; and that every Master, or other Person, who shall have the Charge of a Ship, or other Vessel, who shall offend in any or either of the said Cases, shall, for every such Offence, forfeit Ten Shillings.

And be it further Enacted by the Authority aforesaid, That from and after the Time

Time aforesaid, no Ship, or other Vessel whatsoever having on Board any Quantity of Gun Powder, exceeding the Weight of Fifty Pounds, shall come higher up in the said River than the White-Horse, or the Marsh-End, until the said Gun Powder be discharged, under the Penalty of Five Pounds Sterling, to be forfeited by the Master, or Person who shall have Charge of every such Ship or Vessel.

And be it further Enacted by the Authority aforesaid, That from and after the Time aforesaid, no Ship, or other Vessel, shall continue at the Custom-house Quay, in the said City of Cork, for any longer Time than such Ship, or other Vessel, shall be discharging or loading Goods, and that as soon as any Ship, or other Vessel, is discharged, or laden, she shall depart from the Quay the next Tide after she floats; and that every Ship or Vessel, having a Warrant to discharge, shall take Place of every Ship or Vessel which has not a Warrant for so doing, and that the laden Ship or Vessel, coming to discharge, shall take Place; and that every Master, or other Person having Charge of any Ship or Vessel, refusing so to give Place, shall, for every such Offence, forfeit Forty Shillings; and that the Wa-

Chap. XVIII. ter-Bailiff, or his Deputy, may be authorized and impowered to remove the said Ship, or other Vessel, to some other Place.

And be it further Enacted by the Authority aforesaid, That from and after the Time aforesaid, no Ship or Ships, or other Vessels, shall lie so close in the said Custom-House Dock, or in any other Publick Dock in the said City, so as to prevent any other Ship or Vessel from having a free passage into or out of such Docks, on every Side, under the Penalty of Five Pounds, for every Ship or Vessel which shall block up, or obstruct such Passage, unless it shall appear, that such Ship or Vessel was struck on Ground by Accident, or benipt by the Tide.

And be it further Enacted by the Authority aforesaid, That from and after the Time aforesaid, every Master, or other Person, who shall have Charge of every Ship or other Vessel, lying at Anchor from the North Bridge, to the Black Rock in the said River, shall, at all Times, keep sufficient Hands on board, who shall slack their Cables or Hawsers, as often as shall be needful, for the safe and free Passage of every

other

other Ship, Boat, or Vessel up and down the River, under the Penalty of Ten Shillings for every Neglect thereof.

And Whereas several laden Ships may want convenient Births at the several Quays in the said City, where light Ships are made fast, the Masters, or other Persons having Charge of which, may refuse to give Way to such laden Ships to discharge.

And Whereas also several Ships may happen to moor, or lie at Anchor in the said River, so as to obstruct the free Navigation therein; Be it further Enacted by the Authority aforesaid, That from and after the Time aforesaid, the Water-Bailiff and his Deputy, may be respectively authorized and required to give Notice to any such Ship or Vessel, so refusing to give Place to any laden Ship, or obstructing the Free Navigation in the said City, to remove to some other convenient Place without Delay; and that the Master, or other Person having Charge of any such Ship, or other Vessel, who shall refuse or neglect so to do, shall, for every such Offence, forfeit Forty Shillings; and that the said Water Bailiff and his Deputy, may

be

Chap. XVIII. be further authorized and required, upon every such such Refusal or Neglect, to remove such Ship or Ships, Vessel or Vessels, to some convenient Birth, near the Place where such Ship or Ships, Vessel or Vessels then lay, as they shall judge most proper.

And be it further Enacted by the Authority aforesaid, That the several Penalties herein before mentioned, shall and may, upon Complaint being made before the Mayor of the said City of Cork, be recovered and levied in a Summary Way, from the respective Masters or other Persons having Charge of any Ship or Ships, Vessel or Vessels, offending in the Premisses, by Distress and Sale of the Offenders Goods and Chattels, by Warrant under the Hand and Seal of the said Mayor; Half of the said several Penalties to be paid to the Treasurer of the Workhouse of the said City, and the other Half to the Informer, or other Person who shall sue for the same.

And be it further Enacted by the Authority aforesaid, That if any Person shall be sued or Molested, for any Thing done by Virtue or in Pursuance of this Act, such Person

Person may plead the General Issue, and give this Act, which shall be deemed a Publick Act, and the Special Matter in Evidence, for his Defence; and that if a Verdict shall pass for the Defendant, or the Plaintiff discontinue his Action, or be non-suited, or Judgment be given against him upon Demurrer, or otherwise, the Defendant shall have and recover double Costs.

AN ACT

FOR

Building a Stone Bridge from the Quay opposite *Prince's-Street*, in the City of *Cork*, to *Lavit's-Island*, and a Stone Bridge from thence to the *Red Abbey Marsh*, with a Draw Bridge, or Lifting Bridge of Wood, in the Center of the latter, sufficient to let Vessels pass and repass, and also for supplying the said City with Water.

DUBLIN:

Printed by BOULTER GRIERSON, Printer to the King's most Excellent Majesty. MDCCLXII.

AN ACT FOR

Building a Stone Bridge from the Quay opposite *Prince's-Street*, in the City of *Cork*, to *Lavit's-Island*, and a Stone Bridge from thence to the *Red Abbey Marsh*, with a Draw Bridge, or Lifting Bridge of Wood, in the Center of the latter, sufficient to let Vessels pass and repass, and also for supplying the said City with Water.

CHAP. XIX.

WHEREAS there are only two publick Avenues leading into the said City of Cork, which Avenues are narrow and inconvenient.

CHAP. XIX.

And Whereas the making publick Avenues into Corporate Cities, will conttribute to the Ease and Safety of Passengers, the adorning the said Cities, and will be of Use and Benefit to the Publick.

Be it Enacted by the King's Most Excellent Majesty, by and with the Advice and Consent of the Lords Spiritual and Temporal, and Commons in this present Parliament assembled, and by the Authority of the same, That from and after the First Day of June, One thousand seven hundred and sixty-two, it shall and may be lawful, to and for the Mayor, Sheriffs, and Commonalty of the said City of Cork, to build and erect a Stone Bridge, not exceeding in Breadth Elventy-six Feet, over a Branch of the River Lee, running through the said City, from the Quay opposite to the Street called Prince's-Street, on Dunscomb's-Marsh, in said City, to the Northern, or opposite Part of the Island, called Lavit's-Island, and also to build and erect one other Bridge from the Southern Part of the said Island, over the Southern Channel of the River Lee, to the Red Abbey Marsh, in the Southern Liberties of the said City, not exceeding the Breadth of Twenty-six Feet, and that the said last mentioned Bridge shall contain Two Stone Arches,

Arches, and between the said Arches there shall be a Lifting, or Portcullis Bridge, of at least Twenty-four Feet in the clear in Length, in order to permit Ships and Vessels to pass and repass, and that the said Two Bridges, and all Ways and Passages leading thereto, shall always be, and remain publick Avenues to and from said City.

And whereas the said City of Cork, from its Contiguity to the Sea, and the frequent Flux of Salt Water Tides, wants a Supply of Fresh Water, as well for the Convenience as the Health of the Inhabitants thereof.

For Remedy whereof, Be it Enacted by the Authority aforesaid, That from and after the First Day of June, One thousand seven hundred and sixty-two, it shall and may be lawful, to and for the Common Council of the said City, for the Time being, and such Freemen at large of the said City, as shall be elected in open Court of Doyer Hundred, after a previous Posting in Writing of eight Days, on the Exchange of the said City, for that Purpose, and the Person and Persons to be by them appointed, and employed from Time to Time, to enter into the several Grounds of any Person or Persons within the Liberties

Chap. XIX. ties of the said City (Houses, Gardens, Orchards and Yards excepted) and to dig, raise, and make one or more Reservoir or Reservoirs thereon, for the holding and containing Fresh Water, and to dig, cut, and carry any Trench or Trenches, Water-course or Water-courses, from the said Reservoir or Reservoirs, to any River or Rivers adjacent, for the effectual conveying Water to the said Reservoir or Reservoirs, and also from Time to Time to enter upon the said Grounds, to repair the said Reservoir or Reservoirs, Water-course or Water-courses, and also to dig and cut through the said Lands, from the said Reservoir or Reservoirs, and to fix and lay Pipes in and through the same, and in and through all Streets, Lanes, Ways, and Passages, in the said City, for conducting and conveying the said Water from the said Reservoir or Reservoirs, to the several Parts of the said City, the Common Council of said City, and such Freemen at large of the said City, as shall be so elected as aforesaid, always paying to the respective Owners and Occupiers of the said several Grounds, on which the said Reservoir or Reservoirs, Water-course or Water-courses, shall be so made, and in and through which the said Pipes shall be so laid and carried as aforesaid, such Rates or Damages, in Case the

Parties

Parties shall not amicably adjust the same, as shall be adjudged reasonable by a Jury of Freeholders of the County of the said City, to be impannelled at the next Assizes for the County of the said City for that Purpose, by the Sheriffs of the said City, and whose Verdict shall be taken before the Judge or Judges of Assize for the said County of the said City.

Provided no Person shall be on the said Jury, who shall be one of the said Common Council, or one of the said Freemen so to be elected as aforesaid.

And be it further Enacted by the Authority aforesaid, That if any Person shall break, throw down, or destroy any Trench or Trenches, Water-course or Water-courses, so to be made in Pursuance of this Act, or shall make any Hole or Holes through the said Water-course or Water-courses, or shall make any new Trench or Trenches from the said Course, to carry off, or divert the Water from the same, every Person so offending shall, for every such Offence, forfeit the Sum of Ten Pounds, to be recovered by Civil Bill before the next going Judges of Assize for the County of the said City; one Moiety thereof to be paid to the Treasurer of the Workhouse of the said City, for the Use of

CHAP. XIX. the said Work-house, and the other Moiety to the Person who will inform and sue for the same.

And be it further Enacted by the Authority aforesaid, That if any Person shall be sued or molested for any Thing done by Virtue, or in Pursuance of this Act, such Person may plead the General Issue, and give this Act, which shall be deemed a publick Act, and the special Matter in Evidence for his Defence; and that if a Verdict shall pass for the Defendant, or the Plaintiff discontinue his Action, or be nonsuited, or Judgment given against him on Demurrer, or otherwise, the Defendant shall have and recover double Costs.

FINIS.

www.ingramcontent.com/pod-product-compliance
Lightning Source LLC
Chambersburg PA
CBHW030303240426

43673CB00040B/1043